12 R|S   5

D1795410

Famous Feats of Espionage

Famous
Feats of Espionage

Leonard Gribble

Arthur Barker Limited
5 Winsley Street London W1

Printed in Great Britain by
Redwood Press Limited
Trowbridge, Wiltshire

Contents

For Rodney

*whom I remember best without
three rings on his cuffs – because
a secret agent by any other
name is still a spy*

Author's Preface

Espionage has at least two things in common with every other human career. First, luck: determined by a conjunction of time and circumstance, it is able to play a major role in any developing real-life spy drama. It is the factor that no plan, however well prepared and rehearsed, can allow for completely. Second, the spy of exceptional ability, aptitude, application and resource is the one who performs outstandingly, as is true of persons in all other spheres of human activity, and this is the one who thereby becomes the maker of history. There are ample examples in the following pages to demonstrate the truth of this assertion.

In the curtained world of spies and spying there has never been any need for a Women's Lib. movement, for the female secret agent has since earliest times achieved more than mere equality with male rivals by exploiting the advantage afforded by her sex. No better example could be provided than the subject of the first chapter in this book.

Yet it may be that such different female performers as the Jewish girl Judith and the Egyptian queen Cleopatra secured no insignificant advantages for their peoples by the contrived and calculated employment of their looks and feminine personalities. It would also be unrealistic to imagine that Sheba's dusky queen moved around Solomon's domain with her eyes shut.

On the other hand the male spy, with nothing working for him save a carefully manufactured lie, which today is dignified by the description of a cover story, is often a lone actor

1

playing a studied role at a time when the management switches plays in mid-performance. If he is smart he can ad lib as brilliantly as Dr Edward Bancroft two hundred years ago, but even he had to take a stand, when the chips were down, to secure the cash he felt he had earned.

A century before Bancroft a Breton gentleman's daughter could gain vast wealth and even nobility in the fascinating world of the employed secret agent. Today the work is more arduous, vastly more exacting, and incredibly less rewarding. For the truth is that history has absorbed the spy and secret agent, whatever the descriptive tag, like a sponge.

With the passage of the centuries women spies have, for the most part, been shorn of their old-time glamour, and the men of an inflated patriotism, whether genuine or assumed. Spying, after the experiences of two global wars, has become a job for trained artisans who have served their apprenticeship. This applies to both sexes alike. The allure and the excitement of playing a lone role have been exchanged for team membership and a guaranteed security – provided all goes well.

That is why reading about secret agents and spies who were exceptional persons in their own right invariably provides rewarding entertainment for anyone who likes peeping behind the curtain of history and identifying with an actor or actress performing a dramatic role in secret. For the truly imaginative reader even the suspense of the moment can be captured; for the perceptive reader there is always the prospect of discovering a sharp irony; while for all readers the essential drama is absorbing and thoroughly challenging. In the following very diversified feats of espionage all the central characters performing their secret roles, men and women alike, were exceptional as individuals and provide stimulating company in which to mingle. Just as exceptional were the national and international dramas in which they immersed themselves.

1 Why the Lady-in-Waiting Didn't Wait

Only two of the many women in the female-strewn life of Charles II can be said to have captured a permanent place in the wayward heart of the Merry Monarch. One was Nell Gwynn, child of the London slums, and the other was his younger sister, Henrietta Anne, whom he affectionately addressed as Minette.

In May 1670, ten years after Charles had returned to London for what was termed his restoration, both these women played a dominant role in his life. After a year of being recognized more or less as his official mistress Nell Gwynn gave birth to her first son by him. That was on 14 May.

A few days later, following upon a long exchange of letters covering a considerable period, Henrietta Anne sailed from France to present her brother with the outcome of their negotiations. It was to become known as the Treaty of Dover and was in two parts. Only the first part, which was virtually a secret treaty, was to be signed. By its terms Charles agreed to further the conversion of England to Roman Catholicism. This was fervently desired by his Catholic sister and shrewdly stipulated by the other party to the treaty, Louis XIV of France, for whom she was acting. As the wife of Philippe, Duke of Orleans, Louis's younger brother, Henrietta Anne was in a unique position to act as intermediary between the two monarchs. The second part of the treaty was a more diplomatic document. By its terms Charles, whose kingly pockets were empty, would receive some two hundred thousand pounds in cash, the support of six thousand French troops if they were needed when he declared himself to be a Catholic and a further three hundred thousand pounds a year to help defray military expenses in a war against the Dutch. Further, there was a stipulation that Charles would support any claim made by Louis to the Spanish succession. This part of the two-part treaty was to be formally signed the following December, in order to allay any suspicion of secret negotiations.

When Henrietta Anne returned to France the curious treaty was a fact, though one part of it was to remain an unsuspected mystery for a century. Almost more important to Charles was another fact. He wanted very much to see again the lady-in-waiting who had attended his sister. This was a dark-haired beauty with heart-shaped face and softly lustrous eyes that provided a sharp contrast to the Titian hair, cider-apple cheeks, and hazel eyes of Nell Gwynn, at the time very preoccupied with her baby son. It may be assumed that the lady-in-waiting had not waited overlong in displaying her very feminine charms to Charles's roving eye. When informed that she would accompany her mistress to England she had said to Henrietta Anne, 'I have heard a great deal about your royal brother, Madame.' Henrietta Anne, who was formally called Madame at Court because she was the wife of the French king's brother who was always called Monsieur, had given her lady-in-waiting an arch look and remarked, 'Charles has a reputation with the ladies. If I am not mistaken, Louise, he has more than earned it. So be careful.'

Louise Renée de Keroualle had, in fact, been most careful – to be seen by Charles and to appear attractive to him. She had not only the required good looks but also the alert mind of a formidable *femme fatale*. All she required was the opportunity to indulge her fatal charm. That, to her, was more important than a dozen treaties. As for Charles, if he was uneasily aware that the new treaty meant the end of the Triple Alliance, signed two years before between the three

Protestant Powers, Holland, England, and Sweden, he found ample distraction for the moment when he looked at his sister's lady-in-waiting. The open invitation in her warm glance was one he felt he could not refuse. Any deeper qualm was stilled by a very accommodating conscience. He was playing a secret game at which his maternal grandfather had been an expert. Henry of Navarre, in his own pithy phrase, had decided 'Paris was worth a Mass' and as proof changed from Huguenot to Catholic and was crowned Henri IV of France and reigned until a mad monk's poignard found his heart. Charles had readily embraced the Protestant faith in order to secure his occupation of the English throne. He was not likely to jeopardise his kingly status for a paper promise, but he was prepared to make a paper promise of his own in order to receive most welcome subsidies of cash from the wealthy Louis. Very largely this was the reason for that secret treaty. Charles had no wish for it to become generally known and thereby as deadly as the blade in the hands of François Ravaillac. Life could be far too pleasant, especially if one's more intimate hours were shared with such a charmer as Mademoiselle de Keroualle.

Louise de Keroualle was the daughter of a Breton gentleman with an estate near Brest, which was later purchased by the French Government in order to provide the seaport with an enlarged harbour. Her Breton background was revealed by the 'Ker' prefixing the family name, which referred to the enclosed domain on the estate. Similarly today Breton hotels are named Ker-Yvonne or Ker-Mor, carrying on the tradition of land ownership.

Louise had been brought up to realize she had to make her own way in the world and not to rely on a large dowry provided by her father. Her first step towards fortune had been when she joined the household of the Duke of Orleans as lady-in-waiting to the Duchess. Her first step towards fame was when she landed in England and was seen by Charles. She had no idea at the time that she herself was to become more famous in English history than her own sovereign's sister-in-law. As a result of a tragic event she commenced a career as one of the most efficient female spies of the seventeenth century and became the model for all the Mata Haris of more recent times. This was the sudden death of Henrietta Anne within a month of her return from England. There was a rumour at the time that she had been poisoned by a cup of chicory at the instigation of her husband, a homosexual who wished to be free of her. But in fact she died of natural causes on the last day of June. The signing of the diplomatic part of the Treaty of Dover still had to wait until 21 December and in that document no reference was made to religion. So much of poor Minette's effort was wasted.

In the meantime the French Ambassador in London, Colbert de Croissy, sent a dispatch to Louis informing *Le Roi Soleil* of Mademoiselle de Keroualle's considerable success as an enchantress. The Sun King's reaction was to pave the way for the Breton mademoiselle's return to England, this time with instructions as to what she should do on his behalf. She was going to take over where Minette had finished her work as intermediary. She was, in effect, to become the personal secret agent of the French king at the Court of St James. Being what she unquestionably was, Louise improved considerably on her instructions. She journeyed to England in the royal yacht sent to convey her from Calais, and before long was the French king's secret agent in Charles's bedchamber. For his part Charles observed the niceties of the day by having her made a maid-of-honour to his queen, Catherine of Braganta. Thereby Louise had free entry to the private royal apartments at Whitehall. Within a few weeks she was given a splendid and sumptuous apartment of her own at the end of the gallery at Whitehall. The money for this came from the cash supplied by the French king.

Indeed, it seemed to Louise that the opportunity of dipping her slim but firm fingers into Charles's new cash resources was one that had to be taken. She became, in course of time, the most avaricious woman at the English Court. Whereas Nell Gwynn liked money only for what she could buy with it, Louise de Keroualle liked it for the substance it provided in her life. She quickly became greedy and her greed was indulged by Charles presumably because her arts of amusement and entertainment were unique. In time her greed became notorious. When she appeared on the streets of London in her fine coach the Cockney crowds reviled her. Nell Gwynn had an equally fine coach and her house in Pall Mall was for a time the talk of the town, but when she drove through London and was recognized the crowds cheered her. The two royal mistresses were fated to be rivals in the eyes of the public, which took every occasion open to it to show how partisan were its feelings.

It is said that on one occasion when Nell Gwynn was driving towards Whitehall her coach was stopped by a crowd who mistook it for that of the Frenchwoman. Some lusty advice was tossed at the occupant. Nell Gwynn lost her temper and opened the door to show herself. 'You're wrong', she shouted. 'I'm not the French whore. I'm the English one.' It was the sort of sally, pert and bawdy, that had made Nell Gwynn, the Drury Lane orange-girl, an instant success when given the chance to appear on the stage of the Theatre Royal at the age of fifteen.

The two women, the redhead reputed to have been born in Hereford and the brunette from Brest, continued in their dual roles of royal favourites: probably because they were such physical contrasts they could match most of the Stuart moods between them. But whereas Nell had a mission in satisfying the paying customers at the Theatre Royal as well as the monarch with a liking for change in his amours, Louise found her mission was fulfilled in part by supplying Louis XIV with every piece of information she could come by, whether rumour or gossip or a confession from Charles's own rather sensuous lips.

Charles must have been aware of this, for he was no fool, as he proved years later when he personally revealed Titus Oates, the notorious mountebank and bogus discoverer of the alleged Popish Plot, to be both a liar and an arrant rogue. But he was very possibly secretly amused to think of Louis sending him money and instructing Louise to play her part as spy. Charles had a mind that could appreciate the finer points of irony, even if they were missed by the members of his House of Commons, who kept him short of funds as a strict matter of policy, one that had the virtue of being very economic.

The information sent to Louis by Louise involved that power-bemused monarch in an incredible number of abortive negotiations and kept the French Ambassador at the Court of St James working late by rushlight. That harassed man tried to ease his burden by endeavouring to get Louise to send him information direct. But she was too wily for that. She wished to be useful to two kings, not merely one. She knew that Louis had a new favourite of his own, the notorious Louise de la Vallière. Cunningly the young woman from Brittany sought to provide for Louis what her namesake could not, and in time she had her reward.

Two kings found reason to express their gratitude to her. Charles was additionally happy because Louise de Keroualle shared his enthusiasm for horse-racing, which Charles did his best to make the sport of kings. He first took Louise with him to Newmarket in October 1671. Thereafter horse-racing was something else they shared. It was in this shrewd way that Louise became confidante as well as mistress. Whereas Nell Gwynn could not bother to think about or discuss affairs of State, Louise would not only listen, but tender advice readily if it was requested, and of course in this way she subtly strove to further the interests of the king on the far side of *La Manche,* as the French term the English Channel.

Louise was by nature fiercely possessive, but she schooled herself to be discreet about Charles's possessiveness, being well aware of his liking for a pretty face, a trim ankle, and anything connecting the two if the voluminous female garb of the day could be removed. She plotted against rivals in secret, but was careful not to involve Charles directly. There is a painting of her by Lely. It shows the head and shoulders of a shapely brunette with slumbrous but watchful eyes, small features, and dark hair curled across her forehead from both sides. She could have realized that at times, when looking at her without passion, Charles found in her beauty a reminder of his sister who had employed her, and even his mother who had given her Gascon looks to Minette, and Louise might have been shrewd and perceptive enough to use for her own advantage those memories that were the richest items in a sentimental king's private treasury. For throughout the bad years of exile Henrietta Anne had been a bright star in her brother's gloomy firmament. She had been born at Exeter in the year his father suffered a severe reverse at Marston Moor. In that same dark year his mother, Henrietta Maria, had returned to her native France and never again saw her ill-starred husband.

Perhaps when looking at the face of Louise de Keroualle in repose Charles thought of that uncomfortable night spent in the Boscobel oak and of the next few days' riding to reach Shoreham and a rough sea passage in a cockleshell collier to Fécamp, on the coast of Normandy. At that time Louise had been a child of two. Now Minette was gone, and her death at Saint-Cloud, near Paris, remained to him something of an unexplained mystery. Gone too was his mother, who had been married to his father by proxy in May 1625, shortly after Charles I had succeeded James I. He had brought his mother to England in 1660 at the time of the Restoration, and for a while kept her close to him at Somerset House. But she had gone back to France, wanting to be near Minette. She had died at Colombes in the summer of 1669, while he was corresponding with his sister.

They were bitter-sweet memories and only Louise de Keroualle had the magic of inducing them to return in his contemplative moments. The illiterate and warm-hearted Nell could not compete with her rival at this sentimental level. She could not write a letter, and she could only scrawl a barely decipherable 'E.G.' at the end of some lines written for her by a paid companion. Louise could write her own missives to the French king. Looking at her, Charles could remember that her dead mistress had been the patroness of both Racine and Molière.

He certainly indulged her extravagance and rapaciousness, perhaps believing that in this way he could ensure that she would always temper her writings as Louis's secret agent in a way that would not imperil the flow of welcome gold from Paris to London. In support of this one can consider the time consumed by Louise's correspondence as a spy at Court. She wrote nothing to make Louis impatient, and possibly it was largely due to this that the notorious conversion clause in the secret Treaty of Dover never came into effect. With her native perception she came to realize that Louis was interested primarily in military projects, while Charles's chief preoccupation as a monarch was the establishment and continuity of monarchical power. Indeed, without Minette to prod him, Charles sought to achieve his ends by promoting a policy of religious toleration that was too enlightened for many of his ministers and subjects. As for Louise, the accumulation of wealth was her real religion, one best served in the bedchamber rather than on her knees in church. She strove to keep the truth of this from both of her royal masters, and in so doing became, three hundred years before the term was coined, a double agent. But her success won her an assured place in history.

Not surprisingly Louis was anxious to help her in her endeavours. At his request Charles agreed that she should be naturalized as an English subject. This gave her dual nationality, which added considerably to her sense of personal security, as did the arrival of a son in 1672. Charles agreed that the child should be named Charles Lennox. In the following year the mother was created Duchess of Portsmouth. The Breton mademoiselle had become a member of the nobility of England. It was not enough. She took occasion to point out that France was lagging behind England. Louis showed his appreciation in the way expected of him: the English Duchess of Portsmouth was also created the French Duchesse d'Aubigny. Former mistresses of Charles, like Lady Castlemaine, could only sniff their disdain and think about their own lost opportunities.

To Nell Gwynn the power play with titles was a joke. Her son by Charles was Duke of St Albans. As a good mother, she had put her child before herself: Louise was much more designing and grasping. Little Charles Lennox was not ennobled until 1675, two years after Louise became a double Duchess. But she saw to it that he became a double Duke, of Richmond in England and of Lennox in Scotland. And in doing so she subtly strove to demonstrate her supremacy as a royal mistress. For by this time she was mentally alert to the importance of imputation and inference in words of any kind used officially at Court.

There had been a Duke of Richmond and Lennox previously, but he had died as recently as 1672. He had been a handsome and cavalier character who had dared to run off with one of Charles's mistresses, Frances Teresa Stuart, a maid-of-honour to Queen Catherine. Frances had been both gay and irresponsible, which was why she had attracted Charles. She ran off with the Duke of Richmond to the Continent, where the days of wine and roses lasted barely four years. Then she came back to England and demonstrated that her good looks included a very cool cheek. She also displayed considerable nerve. She brazenly presented herself at Court and, to the chagrin of many, was amusedly accepted by Charles, who admired courage of any kind, whether in a racehorse or an ex-mistress. She was only a year older than Louise. Now the title of the man she had run off with was bestowed on Louise's infant son, whose mother had chosen for her motto *En la rose je fleuris*. It is still the motto of the infant's present-day descendants, the family of the Duke of Richmond and Gordon. But Frances Teresa Stuart had her own small triumph which Louise could not take from her or dilute. She became the model for the now traditional figure of Britannia which appeared on copper coins.

The process of ennobling Louise and her offspring did nothing to change the attitude of the English people and Parliament towards her. If anything the Duchess of Portsmouth became more thoroughly detested than Mademoiselle Keroualle had been. She acquired few friends and when away from Charles lived a very contained life, devoted to the amassing of a fortune of nearly six hundred thousand pounds. She settled for cash and security rather than the hollow approval of any false friends and hangers-on to be picked up in the purlieus of St James's. With the money she acquired property, both in England and France, and became as keen a bargainer in cash deals as she had proved in selling state secrets and court rumours. Writing to Louis and keeping Le Roi Soleil *au fait* with the temper of the times in London became, instead of a mission, a hobby. It was one she enjoyed to the full, and there is little doubt that for years she was the best intelligencer in Europe. Louis was at all times kept informed and up to date on how politics were shaping in England and how changes might occur. For all that time Louis was never in doubt that his subsidies to Charles were being earned quite strenuously by the Duchess of Portsmouth, who was making sure that a goodly part of the cash was directed by Charles towards her lavish White-hall apartment.

There was a decade between the creation of the Duke of Richmond and Lennox and the death of the boy's father. In those ten years Louise was often hard put to maintain her position at Court. Only Nell Gwynn, who continued as an actress playing bawdy roles at Drury Lane until 1682, remained a real threat in Charles's favours, and she was loved by Charles for her unselfishness as an opportunist, a quality lacking in her French rival.

To the end of his life Charles retained the attentions and caresses of the two mistresses who for more than fifteen years shared his bed and bounty, but when he lay dying it was the busty one-time orange-girl who filled his thoughts, and almost his last words were an exhortation to his brother James, Duke of York, to look after Nellie. To his lasting credit, James did his best to fulfil his brother's desire. Nell Gwynn was given a pension, but she required it for only two years after Charles's death, for in 1687 Mistress Eleanor Gwynn passed into history.

Alone on her own stage remained Louise de Keroualle, all that was left of the notable age of Restoration Court drama that had revolved round the person of the king. True, James II tried to give the English people an example of what a Catholic king should be, but the image had little shine in their eyes, and his efforts to implement the still secret clause of a treaty signed on 22 May 1670, and to which he had not been a party, were doomed to fail. Indeed, they failed so dismally that his nephew, the Duke of Monmouth, led an army, albeit of ill-equipped yokels, against him. By that time the Duchesse d'Aubigny was comfortably settled on her estates in France. Following Charles's death she had been received civilly by his brother, but with little warmth.

James was a king prepared to make his own mistakes and with no wish to be aided by his dead brother's mistress. Moreover, it is possible that James, more of a real family man than his brother had ever been, eyed with not a little suspicion any overt act by the Duchess of Portsmouth to continue her role of secret agent for France. He was a man in dire need of friends, but not ones who could bring in their train a whole retinue of enemies.

Accordingly, it was not a great while after Charles's death that the Duchess of Portsmouth decided to cross the narrow seas and live as the Duchesse d'Aubigny. Back in France, she had to pay the price of her former success as a spy. She was not encouraged to play any significant role at the French Court. Retirement from a role that had assured her a place in the history of the seventeenth century now awaited her. However, in the event retirement proved a lengthy business, for she did not die until 1734, not quite half a century after the death of the English king who found her not only desirable, but irreplaceable for a curiously complicated number of reasons. She was eighty-five, an age when beauty has become a fugitive even for such a *femme fatale* as Louise de Keroualle.

She died nineteen years after Louis XIV, for whom she had proved a successful secret agent beyond his best hopes; in a year when the battle of Blenheim had been history for thirty years and Queen Anne, the last Stuart monarch to reign in England, had been reposing in Westminster Abbey for twenty.

A third of the eighteenth century had passed: one in which espionage and secret agents and spies were to become professional labels for men and women alike during years of great social and military revolutions.

No one had prepared the way for the coming of the professional woman spy more certainly and dramatically than Louise de Keroualle, and no female spy received greater rewards in cash and kind than this girl from Brittany who,

13

shortly after leaving her teens, became one king's mistress and the hireling of another. Just how much she affected the course of European history can never be known for certain. But one thing is sure: she did, at times convenient to herself, slow or quicken the process of reporting on her findings as a secret agent and so affected the tempo of events. She did, most assuredly, counsel Charles upon certain affairs of state, but just how such advice was weighted in historical quality cannot be truly assessed. Certainly she was determined to remain where the money was, and as she with her long youthful perspective saw it, that was close to the throne; and the closest she got to that was in Charles's bed, which proved close enough.

Whatever else she did, either for Louis or against her adopted country, she certainly worked to keep Charles with French money in his pockets and supported by a throne that was never too comfortable for a Stuart. In this she succeeded, and then she had to live for half a century with the memories created by her success. Even she must have felt daunted at times as, from a window of her crumbling *château,* she sat pensively growing old and watching the world heading towards greater changes than it had ever seen in the past. She drew her last breath in Paris on a November day when mist shrouded the Seine. The king who had possessed her for fifteen years would not have recognized the grey-haired woman had he passed her open coffin.

2 The Inventor Was a Triple Agent

Forty years after Louise de Keroualle's death there was an American woman in London who opened a waxworks which for a time became not only popular but fashionable. Her name was Patience Wright and she came from New Jersey. She was a likeable, intelligent woman with a pair of sharp eyes that observed the world's wagging with a slightly amused expression.

At the peak of her waxwork show's popularity she was known personally to George iii. Indeed, she was invited to Court as an example of the kind of nice young woman the Colonies produced. She even advanced democratic principles to the extent of calling the king George and his queen Charlotte. But the nice young woman from the Colonies was not so ingenuous and naïve as she appeared to fashionable London Society. The owner of the popular waxwork show was a secret agent. The man for whom she was spying and to whom she was sending periodic dispatches was living in Passy. His name was Benjamin Franklin.

The son of an English immigrant to the American Colonies who was a tallow chandler, he had started his adult life as a printer and publisher of *The Pennsylvania Gazette*. Within ten years he had become deeply intrigued by and interested in scientific research, and had achieved some measure of fame by inventing the lightning conductor in 1749. When he came to England as an agent for Pennsylvania in the dispute with England about the Colonies he very naturally made the acquaintance of men with similar scientific interests. One was a chemist, Edward Bancroft, MD, FRS.

In Bancroft the American found a kindred spirit who shared his interests in meteorology, ocean currents, and the scientific aspects of agriculture. Beyond these scientific interests the two ventured on uncertain ground. However, the more friendly they became the more they were able to argue as friends. Bancroft saw few flaws in British politics and tried to make his American friend perceive a point of view to which Franklin was growing each month more hostile. In turn Franklin endeavoured to show his British friend why progressives in the Colonies were shaping their ideas in a way that must inevitably mean secession from the mother country, even at the cost of violent revolution. The two men interested in science argued the subject to and fro, pro and con, and in the end agreed to differ while each accepted that he could respect the other's view-point.

When Franklin returned to America he promised his new friend that he would look him up when he came back to Europe. 'Then you will be coming back?' Bancroft smiled quizzically. 'Oh, I'm sure I shall,' said Franklin. He sounded like a man very certain of his own words, as indeed he was, for he was not only in Europe within a few years, but working on a secret mission to France. This was to arrange an alliance between France and the American Colonies, for it was by this time more observable in America than in Europe that the differences between Britain and her American Colonies could only be resolved by the latter declaring their independence of the mother country. Any such unilateral act, as it would be described today, would be resisted. In short, war was inevitable.

While the Americans would have sufficient manpower to supply regiments for war, they would require more cash than they could raise as well as weapons that would enable them to wage war. As Franklin spelled it out to the French who listened to him, the Americans wanted to be sure of having active help when the crunch came.

The man who could decide the role France would play in

such an event was Loüis XVI, who had no liking for the English and would prefer to see them engage in a costly war they might lose, but who, at the same time, was very cagey in the matter of how he committed his treasure and his resources. Indeed, there was a growing spirit in France that suggested some of the people might be thinking along parallel lines to the American Colonists and Louis did not wish to encourage them. Accordingly he played for time. He told Franklin, 'I must have an independent inquiry made to satisfy myself about conditions, monsieur. While France is friendly to your cause, she cannot commit herself to a firm decision without resolving any natural doubts that arise.'

Franklin knew what was meant. He held himself in patience while a certain emissary of the French king known as Baron de Kalb made arrangements to sail across the Atlantic. He departed with introductions to a number of prominent Americans. While he was provided with a cover reason for the trip, it was the secret meetings with the persons listed by Franklin that would provide the real purpose of the journey.

In Passy Franklin continued a formidable correspondence with the woman from New Jersey who was acceptable at the British court. While Franklin waited for the outcome of the French mission to the New World he worked on a detailed build-up of current conditions in Government circles in London, based on information provided by Patience Wright. One day he thought of his friend Dr Bancroft, who had now received acclaim in scientific circles as the inventor of a new process for dyeing. It occurred to the American that the friendly Bancroft might very well become a useful emissary carrying papers between Patience Wright and himself, for men of science were never hindered in their travels. Indeed, it was a day and age when not only scientists, but the ordinary civilian, was deemed to have no part in operations conducted by generals and their armies engaged in military campaigns. A war was a business of blood and violence conducted by armies. It did not in theory affect civilians except as innocent victims.

During the American War of Independence this was a

theory that broke down in practice. Indeed, it was a war in which the civilian for the first time lost his hitherto historic role of innocent onlooker. Too many became active participants or spies out to gather important information necessary for the conduct of a military campaign. But when Franklin wrote to Dr Bancroft the American Colonies still hesitated on the brink of the abyss. They too awaited word from Franklin. As the weeks passed Louis became more impatient for the return of Baron de Kalb. Before his arrival in Paris with the information wanted by the French king and his ministers Bancroft was in Paris and talking to Franklin in spirited terms about his new invention. Franklin appeared very interested and wanted to know all the other could tell him about it. Edward Bancroft reacted enthusiastically, and in turn inquired of his American friend how events were shaping in North America. Franklin endeavoured to be honest, but strove not to pass on information that he considered particular to his purpose in being in Paris. Bancroft, in reply, sounded sympathetic. When he took his leave he promised to act as courier for the American and take back to England with him letters Franklin might have for his personal friends in London.

It was some days before Bancroft called for the letters. 'I've been taking a short holiday,' he told Franklin. 'I always find Paris stimulating, and French scientists have progressive minds, as I'm sure you appreciate.' What Franklin did not know, and so could not appreciate, was that the mild-mannered Dr Bancroft had been culling knowledge from French sources as to Franklin's intentions in Paris.

'Will you be back in Paris before long?' Franklin inquired.
'Oh, yes, I am writing a book,' the other explained. 'It is a philosophical work, and I have promised to let my French friends see the draft I have in London.'

Thus began a period of ferrying to and from Paris for the energetic Dr Bancroft. When war came eventually the outcome of the Baron de Kalb's activities in North America and of Franklin's own persuasiveness helped Louis to make up his mind the way the American wanted it. Indeed, no better emissary of the new Continental Congress could have been chosen for the mission to France, for he had been one of the group in Philadelphia who had framed the Declaration of Independence, which, although in Louis's royal ears it sounded truly alarming, at least assured him that the Americans were treading a path of severance from England from which they would not stray. Indeed, his eventual agreement to supply money and arms was to ensure that they should not be able to. Louis, like most of his Bourbon ancestors, had wanted to be certain that the power of Britain to wage war on the Continent of Europe was reduced to what he considered safety limits for France.

Franklin was shrewd enough to realize the value of this hidden purpose to further the interests of his fellow-countrymen. He had been living in the cities of Europe long enough by this time to understand that one was seldom provided with the real reason for the kind of politics one encountered. The policy makers in Europe were like gamblers hedging bets. The author of that eye-opening tract *Poor Richard's Almanack* quickly learned the knack. When he had done so he was even more valuable as the emissary of a young country describing itself as the United States of America.

The fifteenth child of a tallow chandler now began to make arrangements for keeping Louis up to his promise of aid and also for acquiring the latest intelligence from London as to the English Government's intentions and the movements of armies. He became what today would be called a spymaster, and his most valuable spy, he considered, was the softly spoken inventor who dabbled in philosophy. Certainly during the years that followed Dr Bancroft was an invaluable aide to Franklin, a friend always ready to undertake a journey when requested, one on whom he could rely to be discreet in certain eventualities and who could be trusted to undertake any mission he had promised to accomplish.

It is uncertain whether Edward Bancroft had ever had the occasion or the opportunity to peruse Franklin's *Poor Richard's Almanack*, published two years before Louise de Keroualle died, and more than forty years before a cargo of tea was dumped in the harbour of the town where Franklin first saw the light of day. But if he had he must have been struck by a philosophic passage which was actually an exhortation to someone of his quietly devious and secretive temperament. 'Dost thou love life?' the young printer had written. 'Then do not squander time, for that is the stuff life is made of.'

Edward Bancroft lost no time, after becoming persona grata with the man working in Passy for the cause of the men Paul Revere had ridden to warn, in becoming a double agent – without Franklin's knowledge. Indeed, Franklin was, at this time, fully absorbed in concluding the terms of alliance by which France officially espoused the declared aims of the colonies in rebellion. If the Baron de Kalb had brought back satisfactory information to Louis, it was Franklin who helped the royal student to accept the logical conclusion one arrived at when considering it. The word was given for food and arms to be shipped to aid the forces gathered under the world's latest national flag, the Stars and Stripes, for the new egalitarianism among the thirteen colonies in revolt did not allow one to have precedence or prominence over another. Louis was due to experience a savage backlash from this manifestation of popular will in little over a dozen years when the Paris mob stormed the Bastille and a very different style of revolution was brought into fashion. But in the late seventies of the eighteenth century the future for Louis and his Austrian queen, Marie-Antoinette, was clouded only by the smoke of guns being fired three thousand miles distant. By the time that smoke had blown away the future for the Bourbon dynasty was too close to be avoided, and ironically the first shots that spelled doom for the entire *ancien régime* in the land that sent Lafayette to fight with the Americans were fired at Lexington.

What France received in return for the loan of the Marquis de Lafayette was the idea of supplanting the Bourbon lilies with a red, white, and blue tricolor, the colours of the Stars and Stripes. No one bothered to point out the singular lack of originality of the colours chosen for the American flag. They were those of the older flag that had triumphed at Blenheim and Quebec. No modern emergent nation would permit such a lack of historical good taste.

Lafayette returned to France full of ebullience and effusion for revolution. He lost his stomach for it, however, when it was not performed according to Anglo-Saxon precepts. He was appalled and disillusioned when the heads of Louis and Marie-Antoinette dropped into the guillotine's basket to shouts of frenetic approval from a gloating mob. Had he not escaped his own head might have followed theirs, but escape merely led to capture by Austrians who taught him how much they disapproved of having the head of their royal princess rolling in a Paris square among unmentionable garbage. It took Napoleon to rescue him, more than twenty years after Washington had crossed the Delaware, when a new style in dictators and crowned heads was about to be the successor of the Reign of Terror.

The Americans repaid their obligation to Lafayette by becoming involved in a second war with Britain at a time when the former mother country desperately needed all her troops to take on the armies of the striding Colossus from Corsica, and they carefully did not end hostilities until the Eagles of the *Grande Armée* were beginning to look unnaturally plucked and forlorn.

Just as the tumbrils and Dr Guillotine's sharp and methodical axe were concealed in the future from the gaze of Louis, so the balding man with straight dark hair, rather in the style of a modern hippie, who sat watching the slow march of events from his home in Passy, could see nothing of the legacy he was bestowing on a king who had received him with cordiality and even a show of affection.

The one man completely unconcerned with loyalties and causes, and who was doing what and for which reason, was Dr Edward Bancroft, who could debate in sprightly fashion on the rights of man and personally did not give a figurative fig for them, for he was devoting all his energies to furthering his career as a successful triple spy. Being a mere double agent, working for Franklin as well as the British, did not satisfy his will to achieve. He wanted to perform for the

French as well. To this end he kept up his journeys between Paris and London much to the satisfaction of Franklin who, after making sure that the food and arms had been supplied to the forces of Congress, was pressuring Louis to complete his promise and send money.

Getting money out of anyone, be he king or peasant, always demands finesse and extended patience if one is not to provide an excuse to have the deal called off. What Franklin was working for was a veritable jackpot among diplomatic loans. He wanted forty million French livres in cash and another ten million as an outright gift. A puzzled Louis was beginning to realize that egalitarianism never comes cheap. What he never had the chance to understand was how high the price would climb: at any rate, for a head that had had a crown fitted to it. So Franklin had plenty to occupy his mind and time.

The comings and goings of Edward Bancroft with his manuscripts and letters from Patience Wright and his tales of who was proposing to invent what were no more than details to fill in a day's few idle moments. Had the telephone been invented Bancroft would never have got inside the front door. As it was he made himself available, always with good grace, and divested himself of all kinds of chit-chat and rumour. Franklin listened attentively, because there might be a kernel of startling truth under the husk of expansive narrative, and Bancroft was cunning enough to drop a hint of something interesting and to accompany it with a guileless expression of frank incredulity.

It worked well enough. Franklin certainly garnered information that helped him in his dealings with the French and, in a more long-term view, gave him something to dispatch to North America that could possibly be of value to the men in Philadelphia who were quarrelling about most things in which politicians in every age find reason for argument and debate.

The truth was the war in North America got along fairly well on its own, shaping like most wars, with setbacks and victories and periods of frustration, with the fighting men becoming cynical about the men who guarded the locked treasure chests. The farmers wanted to get back to their fields, the shopkeepers to their stores, and the bankers to their tills and vaults.

Meanwhile Edward Bancroft was making his runs between London and Paris and by the employment of nimble wits and a sharp intelligence managed to supply Franklin on the one hand and Lord Suffolk and Lord Wentworth on the other with documents and verbal information that proved in the main satisfactory. What only the inventor knew was that he was acting for both sides. He kept up an incredible deception, and although there were times when his rather smooth operations seemed a trifle too smooth to a suspicious George III, he never made the mistake of being caught in an actual and provable deception. He played his game so well that he was acceptable in Whitehall and discovered that he could demand direct access to the royal presence. George III was always ready to hear news that he was flattered to think was designed specially for his royal ear.

The pinch came when Bancroft extended his field of operation to offer to spy for the French, who were toying with lending the Irish aid for an uprising against the British Crown. Bancroft had no love for the Irish, but French money was as good as American dollars or English pounds. Before he left on a journey to Ireland some of his French contacts, who distrusted him and thought to put Franklin on his guard, dropped word in Passy that Dr Edward Bancroft was really an English spy, using his friendship with the American as a useful cover. Franklin laughed at the idea.: 'No, my friend,' he told the confiding French informant, 'you've got it the wrong way round. Bancroft visits me to give me what he has learned in England. Why, he has provided me with movements of troops and ships and decisions taken by Government Ministers.' Franklin would not believe that his friend was deceiving him. At least, he did not purport to believe it, and there has been nothing found ever to suggest that he thought otherwise in private. But the truth was Franklin was being cleverly deceived by a man he believed he was using. Bancroft was even using Franklin as a source to provide him with information about French intentions, for he knew the French thought a great deal of the bluff-man-nered American who represented the leaders of a revolutionary army that was winning a war against the British and so doing the work the French were unable to perform for themselves.

Of course, if communications had been faster Bancroft would have been unmasked speedily. But a great deal of water was to flow under the Seine bridges before a man with a doubt could resolve it readily by picking up a telephone and asking a few questions. More often than not two hundred years ago a doubt remained with one until it was forgotten or was answered by seeming chance. Posting letters that had to cross frontiers was an extremely fortuitous affair, often depending on luck if the missives ever arrived. Even sending a letter by courier did not guarantee its eventual arrival, and often when it did reach the person to whom it was addressed it arrived too late to have much point.

It was because Bancroft overcame the more obvious objections to the chancy postal arrangements of his day that he continued as a successful spy. The claim has been made that the material he took to Franklin was, more often than not, specially supervised and approved by either Lord Wentworth or Lord Suffolk working with the approval of George III. The British Treasury was providing him with a regular salary of a thousand pounds a year for his unusual services, which was no mean sum two hundred years ago. How much Franklin paid him is not known, but it is certain that he was receiving a comfortable income from the American who professed to value the work Bancroft was performing for the American cause. There was a notable occasion when his spy's stipend from the Americans was delayed. This annoyed him as a man who believed in using time to advantage and in not being dilatory. He wrote Franklin a letter of reproof for this failure to reimburse him for 'his dangerous espionage exploits' undertaken at his American friend's behest. The result was a responsive reply that was reassuring, for Bancroft continued his work as hitherto. He must have been a man who, behind his straight face, concealed a truly puckish sense of humour, for he was not merely playing both ends against the middle, he was playing them against both opposite ends.

Bancroft was still operating when the war in North America ended with the capture of Cornwallis at Yorktown. Not unnaturally Benjamin Franklin was authorized to go to London to attend the final peace negotiations. Bancroft operated unabashed, and when Franklin returned to France as the first United States Ambassador to that country he continued cheerfully to help his excellency with the provision of items of intelligence that were considered useful if not vital in the uneasy days of peace.

The French continued somewhat sceptical of his value as an employed secret agent. The Irish trip had not been a shining success. Bancroft had returned from that country with a fancy and rather inflated expense account and the disappointing information that there was very little likelihood, if French forces landed in Ireland, that the Irish would rise in sufficient numbers to guarantee victory in a joint campaign. The French paid grudgingly for this crushing of their high hopes.

Today it is generally believed that Bancroft was best serving the British when he produced that report on his return to France, and there can be little doubt that Whitehall knew before the Tuileries what Bancroft's report would contain. The French did not employ him again, but then he did not expect they would.

He expected still less that George III would turn against him, and for what seemed to Bancroft the most unlikely of reasons. As a man who was prepared to gamble his life on the way he lived it, the triple agent felt it not unreasonable that he should gamble more lucratively on some of the results of the information he carried. It was from Franklin himself that he learned of certain speculations in concerns that would grow in value with the conclusion of hostilities in the former colonies. Bancroft purchased some of the shares. This could not be done secretly, however, and the news of his spending some of his money to buy shares in what had become wholly American operations, while it pleased Franklin, gave George III reason to mistrust him. The next time he arrived in London the monarch refused to see him. This was tantamount to dismissal, as he discovered when he learned that Suffolk and Wentworth had been instructed to discontinue using his rather unique services.

The man who had promptly written a letter of complaint when the American payment he expected was slow in arriving just as promptly complained to their lordships. They afforded him an interview and explained the situation.

'I cannot accept it,' Bancroft informed them.

Suffolk glanced inquiringly at Wentworth, who shrugged.

'Leave things with us,' the inventor was told.

'Before I do I'd like to be reassured that my interests are in safe hands,' he said. 'As safe as my own.'

Their lordships knew very well what he meant. By this time, after years of espionage work, Edward Bancroft was a man who knew a great many secrets. Some of them could be very embarrassing if an overt act of indiscretion made them public. So without the knowledge, much less the approval, of their king the pair of noble lords made their own secret arrangements to keep Bancroft's mind and mouth fast closed. They sanctioned the regular payment to him of a pension for his past services. The chemist who had invented an established dye process decided it was high time he gave up operating under false colours. He dutifully retired to enjoy gains that quite a few narrow-minded persons would have considered ill-gotten. He even sold his American securities at a substantial profit, which was not surprising. There was a canny streak of the Scot in his physical and mental make-up.

3 The Secret Impersonators

Within a century of Edward Bancroft making the acquaintance of Benjamin Franklin the new nation the latter had done his best to help create stood on the brink of an internecine civil war that was to leave scars that are still apparent as unnatural tissue more than a century later. By the time of the Civil War the status of women in civilized communities had changed drastically. Not surprisingly when their menfolk went to war some of them decided to fight in their own fashion. They offered their services to their respective Governments, Confederate and Union, as spies. Some of them won a sure place in history and for a time were successful in shaping events. Like the famous Rose Greenhow, who gave her life in the service of her beloved South.[1]

At least one female spy for the South donned a Northern uniform to help further her activities. She was the lovely Belle Boyd, who was a *femme fatale* in the popular tradition, one who employed her femininity and good looks to aid her operations as an active spy. Belle was reputed to have the best pair of ankles in the South. Nothing daunted her and neither danger nor personal risk deterred her from what she considered her duty to her beloved Southland. Before she was twenty-one she had been reported in the North as a spy on what are claimed to be numberless occasions. Certainly she had been arrested seven times and imprisoned twice.

Belle Boyd was, in fact, the daughter of a civil servant

[1] See 'The Epic of Rebel Rose' in the author's *Stories of Famous Spies* (Arthur Barker Ltd).

from the North and was seventeen when the first guns were fired at Fort Sumter. She was with her mother in a house at Martinsburg, in Virginia's Shenandoah Valley, when Northern troops entered the town to take over the railroad works. Some tried to force an entry into the Boyd home, and Belle's mother tried to stop them. She was brutally knocked down with a rifle butt. That was too much for a high-spirited girl to take. She ran for a pistol when the invaders were trying to raise the Stars and Stripes over the house. 'Take it down,' Belle ordered the man who had knocked down her mother. He laughed at her. He was still laughing when Belle shot him. He fell dead. Belle was arrested, but when brought to trial was acquitted after the story of the treatment of her mother was told. When she left the court her mind was made up. It remained made up throughout four years of war. She would actively help the South. How she was not sure until some Federal soldiers were billeted in the Boyd home and she overheard their conversation while they were relaxing. She realized that what she had learned quite innocently would be important to the local Confederate commander. She would become a spy.

Belle had no training, but took naturally and efficiently to her self-imposed task. Because of her good looks and gay manner she had at no time difficulty in getting young men to work with her and to act as her couriers. J. O. Kerbey, who was sent into the South to act as an *agent provocateur* by Edwin Stanton, the Union's Secretary of War, was once grateful to Belle Boyd for the help she unwittingly afforded an enemy. Kerbey later described appreciatively her 'lithe and graceful figure' and her 'light, rather fair complexion and hair inclined to be strawberry blonde.'

At the time he met her Kerbey was in a Northern prison as a captured Confederate. His purpose was to pick up any useful information from the discussions among real Confederate prisoners. It was rumoured throughout the prison that after his 'capture' Kerbey had been sent to that prison on orders direct from the Secretary of War.

One day he was surprised to see standing in front of his filthy cell a young woman who took his breath away. It was

Belle Boyd, who had been caught and imprisoned for being captured behind the Union lines in a Northern uniform. She smiled at the man with the manufactured reputation as an unremitting enemy of the North.

'Hello,' she said, 'I've heard about you and I wanted to see for myself the man who was sent here on Stanton's express order.'
'Why?' Kerbey asked.
'I think I can get you out,' said the amazing young woman with the smile that could make a man's heart lurch.
'How?'

When she told him Kerbey was amazed at the way she applied herself to her activities as a secret agent. Before long he was planning with her how he should escape disguised as the Negro who brought the prisoners' meals. First Belle persuaded other inmates of the jail to donate clothing that would look like the Negro's. She secured some corks, which she burned in candle flames. Next she produced an old map from somewhere, but refused to tell Kerbey who had given it to her. With the aid of the map she planned minutely an escape route and drilled Kerbey until he knew it and all the significant place-names by heart. But to Kerbey's surprise the route continued past the Confederate lines and deep into the South, and he realized what a useful asset such a route would be for other Northern secret agents. With Kerbey ready to make the break one problem remained: how to get out of the Old Capitol Prison?

Belle's scheme was for him to change places with the Negro, but on the day before the break was to be made Kerbey was taken to the commandant's office and told he was being released. 'Why?' he demanded angrily. 'This is the only reason I need,' said the commandant, and he produced the order he had received for J. O. Kerbey's release. It was signed personally by Edwin Stanton.

Before he could do anything about what he had learned from Belle Boyd she had been exchanged for a Northern soldier who had been taken prisoner by the Confederates,

She arrived back in Richmond, the capital and seat of government of the South, to be fêted and toasted as a heroine. She told the story which caused laughs in many gatherings in Richmond of how the Union commander whose troops had captured her refused to send her to Washington until a Northern agent named Coleridge came and collected her. 'He's the only man I know,' said the Northern commander, 'who could withstand her charm. He hates all women since he married one.'

Probably her most notable exploit was when she joined one of the Confederate blockade runners trying to get to England with a cargo of cotton for Lancashire's mills and a barrel of money for buying additional war supplies for the South. Belle had agreed to further the cause of the South in Europe.

Before the blockade runner could get clear of the North Atlantic coast it was spotted by a Northern gunboat, which gave chase, firing its armament. Belle is said to have sat on the highest bale of cotton in order to follow the chase closely. When the blockade runner was finally overhauled and brought to a halt a boarding party left the Union warship with the captain in the bows. When he saw Belle his breath caught in his throat. He took her and the Confederate captain prisoners. However, he remained aboard the Confederate vessel while it was being escorted to a Northern port.

On the short journey Belle found herself in love – with the Northern captain. She lost no time in plotting with him how to aid the Confederate captain to escape after their arrival in New York, where large headlines announced the capture of the intrepid Southern belle. These were followed by others announcing the escape of the blockade runner's captain.

The Northern captain, whose name was Hardinge, was arrested and court-martialed when he was found to be implicated. He was found guilty and dishonourably discharged from the United States Navy. He took off for Canada to find Belle, who had been deported to the Dominion. In Canada they plighted their troth, in the phrase of the day, and when Belle, still ardently bent on serving the South, sailed for England Hardinge joined her. They arrived eventually in London and were married in one of the city's most fashionable churches, St James's in Piccadilly.

By this time Hardinge had severed any remaining allegiance to the North and worked with his lovely wife to further the cause of the South. He decided to smuggle himself back to Richmond while Belle remained working in London. Just why Mr and Mrs Hardinge separated in this curious fashion has not been explained, but when Belle said good-bye to him before sailing she was saying the words for the last time. Hardinge was dogged by ill-luck and eventually the news filtered back to London that he had been captured and sent to jail. To his Northern captors he was a renegade and a turncoat. The fact that his allegiance had been suborned by a pair of devastatingly bright eyes provided, in the flinty gaze of those considering his crimes, no extenuating circumstance. Indeed, to have married such a delectable thorn in the flesh as Belle Boyd was, to his Federal judges, something that smacked of an opportunism that could have been better employed in a vastly different sphere from a London bedroom. New England pride was pricked and perhaps a streak of latent Puritanism was left festering with an undeclared jealousy. Hardinge was sent, in turn, to some of the most unhealthy prisons in the jurisdiction of his captors. Not surprisingly his health succumbed even when his spirit refused to flinch. What Belle had warned him against at the time he made up his mind to re-cross the Atlantic came most dismally to pass.

For her part she raised money by selling her jewellery in London and tried to negotiate a deal that would buy her husband's release. A goodly sum of her hurriedly raised capital stuck to greasy palms, and she was promised an impressive number of co-operative acts that would bring about her husband's release. In the event he provided his own: he died.

Hardinge's widow, who remained in London awaiting news from the persons who had taken her money, was twenty-one. She was heartbroken when she eventually heard of her husband's death. Her own health suffered, but although in London she was nursed back to strength, she took a long time adjusting herself to what her husband's death really meant to her.

Belle did not return to North America until the close of hostilities. It took her a considerable time to accept her loss, but gradually her vitality and ebullient temperament recharged her with a new kind of forceful personality. Her extrovert qualities reasserted themselves after lying quiescent since Hardinge's death. She became interested in accepting a fresh challenge: one provided by the stage, where John Wilkes Booth, after a highly dramatic professional career that had at times been clouded with politics, had recently performed a piece of historical melodrama that was the outcome of an espionage conspiracy.

Belle had done her best for the cause of the Confederacy while the Stars and Bars had been snapping defiantly in the cross-winds along the Shenandoah Valley, but she was no longer a teenager prepared to shoot a bully who attacked her mother. The years with their mixture of passion and tragedy had changed her, bringing a maturity that faced life intending to evaluate it in new terms. She was not prepared to give her remaining youth to a lost cause. Instead she gave it to a paying public.

The public who lined up at the box office to buy entitlement to sit through her performances acclaimed this newly rising theatrical star. They continued paying when she moved north of the Mason-Dixon Line. Indeed, there were Yankee audiences who came close to idolizing this Southern belle with the strawberry-blonde hair, bright alert eyes, and the kind of soft, slightly husky voice that a different age would label sexy. Belle was still, in her own eyes, an expatriate of sorts when she died in 1901, just forty years after those guns had opened up at Fort Sumter to raise the curtain on a bitter conflict she always thought of, in her Southern way, as the 'War Between the States'.

There was nothing of the Southern belle about Emma Edmonds. She was a Canadian from New Brunswick who had been brought up with no fol-de-rols and fancy fripperies to deck her life, which was austere until her father took the family south to New England. The Edmonds family were great readers of the Bible, which they accepted for the most part quite literally. It was largely due to her Bible studies that Emma grew up with a devout sense of service. She wanted to be a nurse, preferably in Africa.

Indeed, it was because she was seeking information about joining a nursing service somewhere in the region of the Niger that she found herself in New York on the day the newspapers announced that the man who gave America baseball had ordered the firing of those answering guns at Fort Sumter. She did not complete her inquiries in New York and she did not leave to return to her family. Instead, she packed her few things and journeyed to Washington, where she applied to become a military nurse. Abraham Lincoln had just called for seventy-five thousand volunteers to join the Northern armies. Among the first was Emma Edmonds. The first battle of the war was fought at Bull Run, not a great distance from Washington. As a matter of fact, fashionable society in the city decided the battle would be a spectacle well worth watching, like an oversize military tattoo. They drove out to see the defeat of the Southern troops in grey at the hands of the Northern troops in blue.

History wore a wry smile that day. Largely due to the intelligence sent to the Southern commander by Rose Greenhow of the disposition and strength of the Northern forces, and to the military genius of a stumpy little general named Jackson, who that day earned the nickname of 'Stonewall', it was the men in blue who tossed away their arms and fled. Ahead of them rolled the carriages and wagons carrying the sightseers from Washington, most of whom had received a fast bellyful of war and to the quaking of their well-filled insides realized it was not a pretty spectacle of unfurled banners and disciplined troops firing a few rounds and keeping step as they marched to victory. There were too many left lying on the field, and the uniforms of the fallen had a muddy and stained appearance. Moreover, some of the bodies in those uniforms had odd shapes when the firing ceased.

Emma Edmonds found out for herself what war was really like as she worked among the dead and dying. She was one woman who had come from Washington to stay. She worked on the field as a nurse until she had to hide to avoid capture by searching Confederate patrols. When dark came that July day she hitched up her skirts and started walking to Centerville, but the Confederates advanced faster than she could walk. They took the town while she was in it, and she again hoisted her skirts to enable her to climb over a back fence. She reached open fields without being discovered, and walked on through the night as rain began to fall heavily. She continued putting one foot in front of the other even when she had worn out the soles of her laced boots. It was past noon when she staggered into Alexandria. After resting she set out for Washington. This last part of her journey took her two days.

Emma arrived in Washington to find that the routed Northern troops were little more than a drunken rabble. The streets were not safe for a woman on her own, even when dressed as a nurse. At a time when a less resolute woman might have had her faith shaken Emma Edmonds found hers even more firmly established. She returned to service at an army camp near Yorktown. It was here that soldiers of a New York regiment returned with prisoners from a foray. They also brought a rumour that a captured Northern spy had been tried in Richmond and sentenced to be shot. This worried the Northern commander, General McClellan, who discussed the prospect with the chaplain.

'I must send a replacement,' said the general. 'Have you any suggestions? It is imperative that I am kept informed of the enemy's intentions.'
'A nurse might get through Confederate lines,' the chaplain suggested. 'She would be less suspicious than a man.'

McClellan sent for Emma Edmonds and questioned her closely. He found himself being answered by a young woman of spirit with a deep feeling of dedication.

'Can you ride a horse?'
She could.
'Have you any knowledge of firearms?'
She had.

McClellan was a man of his time. After assuring himself that Nurse Edmonds was at least capable to undertake the mission he wished to know her powers of resourcefulness without delay. Accordingly he had a phrenologist probe with his fingers under her hair, feeling the contour of her scalp. What was popularly referred to as her bumps apparently confided to the man feeling the shape of her head that the subject was very suitable to undertake such a dangerous mission. Danger would not deter her, and she would attempt to overcome any difficulty by seeing it as a challenge. Moreover, she should prove responsive to sudden emergency.

McClellan was satisfied. He explained to Emma Edmonds that she was to become a spy, had her take an oath of allegiance for the third time since first arriving in Washington, and then shook her composure by saying, 'You'd better go in disguise. I suggest a Negro.' If the words were a test it was one the nurse passed easily: 'whatever you say, General.' Emma was then sent to the quartermaster and given the clothes of a dead Negro field worker. A camp barber shaved her rather straggly hair until her scalp was bald, then she donned a wig resembling a Negro's head of hair. It had been specially obtained in Washington. The flesh of her head and neck were coloured black and the same dye was rubbed into her arms and hands. When she was ready her disguise was tested. She returned to Yorktown and spoke to the chaplain whose original idea had been changed. Neither he nor his wife recognized Nurse Edmonds in the Negro youth in soiled clothes. Nor did the physician attached to the camp, which suggests that she must have had a very boyish figure.

Her first mission began at half-past nine on a dark and blustery night. In her pockets she carried a loaded pistol and some army biscuits. A few hours later she was behind the Confederate lines, huddled in a corner of a field in the dark, munching some of the hardtack biscuit. The next morning she joined some Negroes who were building fortifications, and was put to work by their overseer. Before it became dark she had written down details of what she had seen, listing the cannon, their various calibres, and the supps of ammunition. She concealed the paper bearing this information under the inner sole of her left boot. She slept better that night.

The next day her disguise was almost pierced. She had bribed a water carrier to change places with her, and she overheard one officer telling another that word had been received that the Southern General Johnston was due to arrive with reinforcements that would bring the total in the immediate area to a hundred and fifty thousand. She was so surprised that she found several soldiers and Negroes watching her with sudden interest. 'Damned if that nigger ain't growing pale,' said one of the officers. McClellan would have approved the speed of her reaction: it was immediate. With a heavy Negroid accent she said her mother had been a white woman and she had always expected to 'come white'. The information was received with laughter. At the first opportunity she concealed herself and touched up her skin with a rag drenched in a weak solution of nitrate of silver. The next day she was given a rifle and told to take the place of a picket who had been killed. She waited until darkness fell and heavy rain was drenching the ground, then left her post and ran towards the Union lines. To avoid being shot by Northern guards, she remained in a trench through most of the night and eventually reached the officer in command of the line nearest to her hiding-place. She reported to him and handed over the rifle she had brought with her. Today it is a carded exhibit in a Washington museum.

The next time Emma ventured as a spy inside the Confederate lines the dark stain had been removed from her flesh. Her Negroid accent had been replaced by an Irish brogue, and instead of a male field worker's trousers she wore the shawl and skirt of a female pedlar. Before many hours she was in the Chickahominy Swamp with a basket of bakemeats, shivering from cold and damp. Much worse – she was lost.

For three days she was too ill to attempt to continue with her mission. It was the sound of gunfire on the following day that sent her struggling to find a way out of the notorious swamp. She came to a house that was deserted save for a Confederate soldier who was dying of typhoid. That was when Emma Edmonds, earning fame as a spy, returned to the profession she had forsaken. She found food and drink for the sick man and fed him. She discovered that he was little more than a boy. He told her his name Allan Hall. Just before he died he gave her his gold watch. 'Please give this to Major McKee,' he whispered. 'He's on Elwell's Staff.'

She roused herself to search the house, and this time found a tin of mustard and another of pepper, some red ink, and a pair of green spectacles. When later she related her adventures as a spy she wrote:

'Of the mustard I made a strong plaster about the size of a dollar. I tied it on one side of my face. It blistered thoroughly. I cut off the blister and put on a large patch of black court plaster. With the ink I painted red lines about my eyes, and after giving my pale complexion a deep tinge with some ochre which I found in a closet, I put on my green glasses and my Irish hood, which came over my face about six inches, and left for the nearest picket line. I felt perfectly safe, for the watch was sufficient passport in daylight and a message for Major McKee would assure me civility at least.'

She took a piece of window curtain as a flag of truce, and the picket who saw it waving turned out to be English. He readily passed her through the lines, but it was to learn that Major McKee was absent until nightfall. She settled herself to wait, and in the interval learned a good deal from soldier gossip around her, particularly the position of a masked battery of guns.

When Emma gave the watch to the major he stared at it and tears filled his eyes. Captain Allan Hall had been his close friend. He offered her a Northern ten-dollar bill, and she made the mistake of refusing it, which aroused the major's suspicions. She allayed them by claiming she couldn't take money for fulfilling the wish of a dying man. She offered to guide a detachment to recover the body, and got away from the sergeant in charge when night fell. Again she reached the Union lines, this time on a Confederate cavalry horse.

Emma Edmonds penetrated the Confederate lines on nine further occasions. At various times, in what were really intervals between spy missions, she returned to nursing. She was employed as a nurse when she suffered a breakdown. Her strength left her and she gave herself up to crying. 'I could do nothing but weep,' she said later, 'hour after hour.'

It has been claimed that two years of privations, hiding in fields and swamps in cold damp weather had undermined her health. This may be true, for she was not the kind of woman to spare herself when given a task to complete. But most likely the reason why her collapse came when it did, utterly and destructively, was that, following upon the privations she had endured, she also endured what was for her a soul-searing experience, one that the nurse could not suffer with the fortitude of the Irish pedlar women she often strove to resemble.

She had moved from the role of spy to counter-spy when she induced a civilian clerk to help her get through the enemy picket line, and this loose-tongued man talked too much. As a consequence she was able to slip a note through the lines to a Union commander, and a trap was sprung. The clerk told her the names of a sutler and a photographer who were working for the Confederacy as he was. Emma Edmonds kept the man talking until they were surrounded by Union cavalry at the time agreed with the female spy. The clerk was taken prisoner and later the sutler joined him in prison. The photographer was less easy to snare. He escaped back to the Confederate lines with a collection of posed Union officers and unposed Union fortifications.

The Union commander was so incensed at the photographer's escape with one of his own pictures that he had the clerk and the sutler shot as spies after a military court had found them guilty on Emma Edmond's evidence. To feel herself in any way responsible for the shooting of two men for behaving as she had affected the Canadian woman deeply. Those executions brought her face to face with a grim new set of realities. She was shocked and mentally disturbed.

Because of this change in her Emma was no longer useful.

In fact, for the men in blue who had used her, she was better out of their way. She could become a hazard and there were, by this time, plenty of trained nurses in the military hospitals. So she was interviewed and afterwards granted a certificate announcing her disability and release from active service. The war was over for one of the most notable female spies who had served in it.

Emma Edmonds went home at last from the long-ago visit to New York to seek details of nursing in Africa. She gave herself to the task of writing her wartime experiences, entitling them *Nurse and Spy*. When the book was eventually published Washington wanted to know who she was. Those who could have explained were noticeably silent. Somehow Emma Edmonds, as a successful spy in the field, lacked glamour, and those were still times when women were expected to be glamorous – at least, when not disguised as a Negro field worker or an Irish pedlar. Emma Edmonds might achieve much, but never glamour. She was much too plain and very much too thin.

4   Kidnapped in London

The youthful-looking Chinese doctor with hair close-trimmed in the European fashion was interrupted in his thoughts as he stared at the swirling sprawl of palm-decorated Hawaii beyond the window of his modest apartment. He turned his head to stare at the door on which someone had rapped smartly. Just for a moment he felt the cold touch of fear stroking his flesh. He knew there were secret agents with orders to watch him and report on his actions. There might even be others with orders to eliminate him as a menace.

The knock on the door came again, as though the person outside was growing impatient. 'I have a letter,' a voice called. 'A letter for you from China.' He recognized the voice as that of the manager of the apartment house. He crossed to the door and opened it, took the letter and said thank you. He closed the door and fixed the latch and went to sit on the small bed on which reposed the suitcase he had been packing. It was a cheap case of cracked leather, for the young doctor was not a man with a well-lined pocket, and indeed the personal clothes stowed in it were few. Most of the suitcase was crammed with pages of neat Chinese characters, with some larger ones at the top of the front page. These spelled out a name. In roman characters the name became Hsing Chung Hui. In English translation this in turn became the Progressive Chinese Society.

The young doctor who was tearing open the envelope of the letter he had just received was its founder. The letter he opened, which had been posted in Shanghai, was from one of the first members of the society he had enrolled. The

writer addressed him as Sun and signed himself Soong and
the letter was dated in the summer of 1894, which was a
momentous year in the history of the Far East.

For one thing, the Manchu rulers of China, with their
avaricious and corrupt mandarins and regional governors,
together with thousands of equally corrupt officials, had just
lost a war, and in the most inefficient manner, against the
enemy they despised, the Shrimp People, (that was the
Manchu name for the subjects of the Emperor of Japan).
Imperial China had taken some punishing blows at the
hands of the well-armed and disciplined troops of the
Shrimp People, who had studied the campaign manuals of
the modern armies of the Western World. As a consequence
the Shrimp People had finally defeated the armies of the
Manchus and had exacted a high price for peace, part of
which had been the surrender of Korea, destined to become
for seventy years a Japanese colony. Thought of that
surrender angered the young doctor reading the letter from
Soong. It had also angered Soong and given him reason to
send the letter. He wrote that all China was mourning the
outcome of the war and that feeling was running high, like
a flood tide, against the rulers responsible for the country's
ignominy and shame: 'Now is the time for us to strike. Now,
without delay. Now is the hour for the revolution we of the
Hsing Chung Hui have preached to change history. Come
home. Return to China. There is no time to lose.'

The characters written by Soong blurred before the eyes of
the man he addressed as Sun, for Sun wanted to believe
what had been written, yet he was not sure. Not of Soong,
but of the other's judgement. If Soong were wrong they
could innocently betray a nation's cause by premature
violence. On the other hand, if Soong were right in his
judgement, then it might be years before a better opportunity arose.

Sun sat on the bed for a long time meditating. He had
been packing his suitcase preparatory to sailing east to San
Francisco. Here in Hawaii members of the Chinese colony
had helped him with funds. Some had joined the Progressive
Chinese Society and had sworn to follow him. They had

41

made sure no secret agent of the Manchus discovered where he had an apartment, and they had helped to publicize the cause among the Chinese in the United States. For although the Hsing Chung Hui was modelled on many Chinese secret societies in existence towards the end of the nineteenth century, it had relatively few of the total of three million members of such societies.

Not all the Chinese secret societies were political. In fact, many more were religious, while others were merely social, and only a few of these mildly reformist, like the well-known Golden Orchid Society, which had received some publicity in the Western world because it was unique: its members were all women, each of whom had taken an oath that she would work to get existing Chinese marriage laws changed. The Progressive Chinese Society had little in common with the older societies except its basic structure. Its aims were frankly revolutionary, and the revolution it preached was not that of constitutional change. It was violent and promised much spilling of blood. The revolt would be against the Manchu rulers of Imperial China. Preferably the blood spilled would be theirs.

This was all the more remarkable when it was remembered that the society's founder was a Christian. But not, it must be admitted, to the doctor who had graduated from the Hong Kong medical school and who had cut his hair and changed his name to Sun Yat-sen when he became the leader of a revolutionary secret society dedicated to the overthrow of the Manchus' tyrannical and oppressive rule. The study of Christianity had, if anything, justified Sun Yat-sen in feeling his purpose was a desirable one. Its tenets encouraged believers to work to improve the lot of the ordinary man, and in China nearly a century ago the life and lot of the ordinary paddyfield coolie was miserable indeed. As an organizer striving to bring about a beneficial change for China's submerged millions Sun Yat-sen saw himself following in the footsteps of Jesus Christ, to him another preacher of a revolutionary doctrine.

Sun had much in common with Soong, whose accepted name at the time was the curious one of Charles Jones

Soong, the name in which he had been baptized by Captain Charles Jones, the master of an American trading ship in which the young Chinese had shipped as a cabin boy. Each of the two young Chinese had provided his own purpose in life. After being educated in Hawaii, Sun, who had been born near Canton, had studied to become a doctor because in that way he could fight mankind's physical ills, while Soong had returned to China after his own baptism to work as a Christian missionary among his own people and heal wounded spirits. Finding each other had been the greatest event in the lives of both up to that time. They found they shared an identical purpose in wishing to bring democracy and decent living standards to the exploited and beggared people who were the virtual serfs of the Manchu war-lords.

When he had read the letter from Soong several times Sun left his apartment and walked through the Hawaiian Chinese colony to meet his friends. He told them of the news from China and of Soong's opinion that the time was ripe for an uprising in which the Hsing Chung Hui should provide a lead. His friends were immediately enthusiastic and proclaimed Soong to be correct with his assessment of the uneasy peace left behind by the Japanese victors.

'I will go with you, Sun,' said one.
'So will I,' said another.

The desire to go with Sun Yat-sen to topple over the Manchus worked like yeast among those he talked to, and Sun Yat-sen soon realized that he had achieved his purpose in coming to them. They had demonstrated how the Chinese in their homeland would react. He took an historic decision.

'Very well, I will join Soong and sail by the first available steamer,' he decided.
'And we are coming with you,' cried those who had helped him to make up his mind.

So the young doctor who lived a secret existence, waiting for the hour to strike when he would declare his purpose in public, bought a ticket to Shanghai and instead of travelling east sailed west to the Chinese mainland. He travelled in the company of the most militant and eager members he had recruited to the Hsing Chung Hui.

The years of hiding himself and working like a spy were about to close. A new age was dawning. Sun arrived in Shanghai full of confidence and buoyed with hope. He also arrived with a slogan, for the long hours of the journey had been spent, often far into the night, by Sun and his companions discussing future tactics and inventing watchwords as well as framing the kind of literature they would start preparing as required propaganda as soon as they had landed. The slogan chosen to epitomize the society's purpose was 'Divine Right Does Not Last For Ever.' Today, in an age when the adman has sharpened his technique to a cutting edge, this scarcely sounds incisively penetrating, but eighty years ago it held a truth – still to be proved in China – that was startling to the point of shattering a listener's equanimity and inducing him to think.

When Sun met Soong the latter came primed with a plan. 'We must go to Canton,' he said. 'There we must make our first active move against the Manchus. We will capture the provincial governor's yamen. Then we shall be in command of the province. Seeing that, the people will flock to us in thousands overnight.' Soong spoke like the missionary he was, convincingly, eloquently, and descriptively.

The yamen was, under the Manchus, the most important centre of government in any province, comprising not only the governor's official residence, which was usually a palace, but within its thick walls the courthouse where justice was administered according to the laws of the Manchu masters. Even more important in the reckoning of scheming insurrectionists, it was within the boundary of the yamen that one found the provincial armoury, which contained guns and ammunition of various kinds, enough to equip an army. Capture of the yamen would mean striking at the nerve centre of provincial government and paralysing it. Political prisoners could be freed from the provincial prisons, and Soong argued that such men with a deep grudge would make willing soldiers who, in turn, would help to convince the provincial troops of the governor that they should desert and join the revolutionaries. It all sounded direct and simple, but Soong had a word of warning for Sun. 'The Manchus have their spies everywhere,' he said. 'We must be very sure that no spy learns of our intentions. There must be no loose talk by any of our members, not even in the hope of gaining recruits to our cause. For the Manchus' spies could destroy us before we make our first vital move.'

It was a sobering warning. The members who heard it decided not to discuss further plans until they had reached Canton, to which they made their way in small groups in order not to arouse suspicion. Assembled there, they hired a room and met for a council of war, with guards posted to ensure that no spy could eavesdrop. At this council plans were made for volunteers to attack the yamen guards and take them by surprise. As soon as the guards had been accounted for the main gate of the yamen would be forced and the armoury occupied. Arms would be distributed to their own members and to any who came forward to join their ranks once the news had spread through the city. With sufficient volunteers under arms the revolution would be publicly proclaimed and the whole of the populace invited to join those who had captured the yamen.

After taking the city the whole of the Canton province would be occupied. Then the successful revolutionaries would carry the rebellion to the gates of the royal city of Peking. By that time China should be in a ferment and the Manchus should be able to read their fate written in words of fire.

However, a further word of caution was offered to the war council. The attack on the yamen must only be made when success would be assured, for an abortive attempt would not only put the Manchus on their guard, it would bring a terrible retribution on the entire populace. That could not be risked. Furthermore, it would be better to wait until the revolutionaries, through their own spies and accomplices, had obtained the latest information about conditions in the yamen and the feelings of the Manchu troops. This would give them a space in which to obtain sufficient weapons for the initial attack on the yamen guards when the word was given.

Delay was opposed by some, but the wiser counsels prevailed. For his part, while Sun chafed at the enforced delay for the reasons given at the council, he could not argue against the wisdom of being fully prepared before the die was irrevocably cast. But he was a young man who had come home. Canton was his province. He ached to free his homeland from the misrule of the Peking tyrants. He took another decision. 'We will not operate as ourselves,' he told the surprised assembly. 'We must henceforth operate only behind a careful front which will deceive the enemy's spies'.

A short time later he formed the Scientific Agricultural Association. It became the headquarters for the Hsing Chung Hui's members working as spies. To provide the 'association' with an impressive appearance, at least on paper, another office was opened in Hong Kong. It was a second local headquarters for the society's spies and agents, who now had instructions to raise funds and recruit likely material as members behind the front of the agricultural association.

The response to the subversive activities of the men working to achieve revolution was more than encouraging. New members who were enrolled gave generously to the society's war chest. One, a friend of Sun's named Lu Hao-tung, became so fervid in his approval of removing the Manchus that he refused to listen to well-meant advice and against Sun's wishes sold some of the land that provided him and his family with their livelihood. He handed over the money to the Hsing Chung Hui. Unrestrained by his wife's tears he also sold some of her jewellery for cash, which he surrendered for the cause.

Secret deals were made in dark rooms in back streets, and stacks of rifles were purchased with boxes of ammunition. Hundreds of pistols were bought, as were supplies of dynamite packed in boxes supposedly holding fruit. The pistols arrived at the offices of the Scientific Agricultural Association in sealed barrels labelled with the single word 'Cement'.

Anticipation brought excitement, and the society's

members enjoyed a sense of happy euphoria simply because they were actively engaged in working towards a longed-for end. The war councils continued and problems raised at them were disposed of by Sun and Soong. For instance, it was pointed out by one member who had taken the trouble to think through a problem that as they had no badge or uniform they would be unable to recognize one another readily when the revolt had started. 'How shall we distinguish friend from foe?' the man asked. Sun Yat-sen took up a pair of scissors and made cutting motions. 'Once the revolution is launched all members will cut off their queues,' he said. 'They are signs of servitude. If divine right does not last for ever, then neither shall the queues of servitude.' He turned to the man next to him at the table where he sat. 'We must not forget to buy enough of these,' he said, snipping again with the scissors he held.

However, the brave plan of the assembled revolutionaries was never carried out. Reports from the Manchus' spies resulted in the Scientific Agricultural Association becoming suspect, or possibly there had been a double agent working with the secret suppliers of arms. But without warning Manchu troops moved suddenly to seal off the entire city of Canton. This news was brought to Sun by a scared Lu Hao-tung.

'You cannot escape through the gates,' he told the stunned leader whose hopes and plans were swiftly in ruins. 'Everyone is being searched and questioned. Your only hope is to get over the wall.'

Sun Yat-sen returned the stare of his friend. 'What went wrong, Lu?' he asked quietly.

Lu Hao-tung could only shake his head and say he didn't know. He told Sun of the rumours he had heard. One was that an informer had gone to the governor. This man could have been a spy planted in the society. Another of the rumours circulating through Canton was that a barrel of cement had been allowed to fall heavily on the river quay. It had burst open, revealing wrapped pistols. Had the false cement barrel been deliberately allowed to fall? There was no

47

way of being sure. The only certainty in that moment was that to remain where he was meant capture and execution for the man who had been cheated of starting a revolution.

Lu Hao-tung volunteered to stay with some other members of the Hsing Chung Hui to destroy the secret files while Sun Yat-sen made his escape. The leader was led by friends to an unguarded section of the massive wall surrounding the city of Canton. They produced a new basket. 'We will have to lower you down the far side,' they said.

It was dark when Sun climbed into the basket which creaked under his weight. Just as his friends paid out enough rope to lower the basket they were joined by a man who was out of breath. Sun had a moment's misgiving which turned out to be justified, for the newcomer brought bad news. The governor's troops had found Lu Hao-tung and four other dedicated members of the Progressive Chinese Society in a room filled with flaky pieces of burned paper. They had been bound and taken away to await trial on the orders of the governor.

Men saddened by the news they had received, and fearful of what the future held for them and their families, took their leave of a leader they lowered into safety. Sun Yat-sen sped away from Canton in the darkness. He was hidden for a time in the house of a friend who afterwards passed him on to another 'safe' house. In this fashion he escaped the searching Manchu soldiers with strict orders to find him. He was still a fugitive on the run when he was told of a petition that had been drawn up by friends of Lu Hao-tung. It pleaded for his life.

Sun knew what this meant. An opportunity had been given to the Canton mandarins to accept a bribe for seeming to be merciful. It was regular practice at the time in the corrupt courts of the Manchu governors. It was Lu Hao-tung himself, however, who robbed the mandarins. When brought to trial he declared, 'I do not beg my life of the Manchus. I accuse them.' He produced a document of his own to replace the petition entered on his behalf by his friends. This document was an accusation and his was the only signature.

He charged the Manchu war-lords with being responsible for all the country's troubles and the loss of the recent war with the Shrimp People.

The court's counter claim was that the document amounted to a confession of the prisoner's guilt. Lu's proud head was struck from his shoulders by the sword of a burly executioner. Then began a great manhunt intended to discover the whereabouts of Sun Yat-sen. Meanwhile orders were given for the imprisonment of the families of Lu and Sun. Lu's relatives were unable to escape. Sun's close relations had already taken the first steps in a flight to Honolulu.

A considerable reward was offered for the capture of Sun and it is believed that he was in danger for at least ten days until he was able to avoid those searching for him among the deltas of the Canton River, where he was threatened by the junks and sampans filled with pirates. Eventually he reached Macao, where for the first time he saw one of the posters offering ten thousand taels for his capture. Living more furtively than a known secret agent, he reached Hong Kong, where the second office of the Scientific Agricultural Association had been set up. In the British colony he was warned that, if the Manchus discovered his whereabouts, they would demand his extradition under the existing treaty terms. To avoid this, and also to cheat the spies in the colony, he again took ship and eventually arrived in Kobe, a city of the Shrimp People. By this time his hair had grown long enough to make a short queue and he cut it short again, Western style. He made inquiries about a passage to the United States, and, still ahead of the spies and secret agents searching for him, sailed for San Francisco, his objective that day when the letter from Soong reached him from Shanghai.

In 1896 he was busy in San Francisco, holding meetings in the Chinatown district, preaching his revolutionary gospel, enrolling members of his secret society, collecting contributions towards another war chest. When he felt he had done enough for the cause among the Chinese in the city of the Golden Gate he started across the United States, heading in the general direction of New York.

The way he made it this journey took three months, and

he was disappointed at the lack of response he had obtained from fellow-countrymen in some of the larger cities. However, he refused to be discouraged, and he kept on the move, well aware that the Manchus must know of his slow progress and the towns and cities he visited. He did not stay very long in New York, but took ship to Europe, arriving in London towards the end of that same year, 1896. He did not know it, but all his suspicions about the Manchus and their spies had been fully justified. Agents of the Manchu warlords were preparing to receive him in London. Indeed, they had evolved a kind of plot that is not unknown to be employed over three-quarters of a century later. They would take him by surprise in the street, kidnap him, and smuggle him into the Chinese Embassy. At a convenient time he would be smuggled from the embassy to a ship which would take him as a confined prisoner back to stand trial in China.

At the end of the nineteenth century this was an hitherto unheard-of infringement of another's country's rights and neutrality, but the Manchus were desperate to remove finally the man who was, in their eyes, more dangerous than a vast host of spies. Once Sun Yat-sen had been executed they could tender their shallow regrets to the British Government, make excuses, perhaps pay an indemnity, and then sit tight, feeling safe from further attempts at unseating them by open revolution.

A friend Sun visited in London warned him of the peril in which he stood. 'You must be on your guard every minute,' he was told. Presumably it was at a time when he was not on his guard that the undercover agents of the Manchus, who had been following him, jumped him and overcame his struggles. He was rushed to the Chinese Embassy and imprisoned on what was virtually Chinese soil. Moreover, no one knew he was there. One of the most deliberate and audacious espionage conspiracies of the nineteenth century had been carried out with no fuss and entirely without the British Government's knowledge.

It is highly probable that Sun Yat-sen might have been smuggled out of the embassy and to a ship in the Pool of London, and then conveyed round the world to China and execution, had not an Englishman employed at the embassy suddenly befriended the unhappy prisoner. He took a message from Sun to the friend who had warned him.

This friend became so alarmed that he was responsible for a report of the kidnapping appearing in the London newspapers. However, a report is not proof. For two weeks there was no diplomatic development, but in that time a great many persons were working in secret, reporters to get more news, detectives making inquiries, specially briefed individuals asking questions in Limehouse and West End clubs. At the end of that time the British Government was satisfied that what the Press was calling an outrage on British sovereignty had been committed. The Chinese Embassy was approached and some blunt words were spoken which Chinese interpreters had no difficulty, but quite a deal of diffidence, in translating. The outcome was that the prisoner was released and one of the most incredible espionage *coups* came to nothing.

By now Sun was news in every country in the world, as were his aims. He remained in Europe for two years before journeying to Japan. The twentieth century opened with the Boxer Revolt in China. But Sun was not making the same mistake, of being premature, twice. In Tokyo he founded the Chung-Kuo Tungmeng Hui, or Chinese League of Covenanters, which came out with a full-scale programme of revolution of its own. That was in 1905. The next year Sun was still being cagey when there was an armed uprising in China. It failed. By 1911 eight more such risings had been started, all overcome by the forces of the Manchus.

On 10 October 1911, yet another revolt erupted at Wuchang, in Hupeh Province. This time it was the Manchu forces that suffered defeat. That was enough. It was a signal for most of the other provinces in South China to rise up against the smitten regime. Sun Yat-sen was in the United States when he heard the news, with another piece that started him on his travels again. The Manchus were trying to raise a loan in London to be used to crush the revolt.

Sun went back to the city where he had been kidnapped and began a hard campaign to ensure that the loan was not raised. When he had this assurance he took ship for China and arrived in Shanghai on Christmas Eve, a date that must have affected him strangely as a firm Christian. This time there had been no kidnap attempt. Secret agents had not been on the lookout for him. Times were changing. The Manchus had been ousted and a Chinese republic proclaimed. On 29 December, five days after his return to his native land, he was elected by a National Chinese Convention in Nanking the Provisional President of the new republic.

But the returned wanderer still felt he had a mission to complete. Some northern provinces adhered to the cause of the Dowager Empress, who had a private army still loyal to her under the command of a war-lord named Yuan Shih-kai. This meant that China was divided, one part empire, the other republic. Sun saw that civil war was inevitable and this was a disaster he wished to avoid.

After designing a new tricolor flag for the young republic he sent emissaries to Yuan and offered a deal. If Yuan could bring about the peaceful abdication of the Manchus the Provisional President would resign in favour of Yuan, ex-war-lord. It was an offer Yuan's pride and vanity would not let him pass up. He would be an emperor in all save name.

On 12 February 1912, after ruling China for 267 years, the Manchu dynasty formally abdicated. The next day Sun Yat-sen kept his promise and resigned as Provisional President. Yuan Shih-kai took his place.

It seemed to the rest of the world that, almost overnight, a modern historical miracle had taken place. China had become a united democracy.

5   The Incredible Masquerade

The story of the Member of Parliament for Darlington in 1910, when that seat was won for the Liberal Party, reads more like fiction than fact, and this is due solely to the curious nature of the Hungarian who had impressed the voters of the Northern town with his personality. He was probably unlike any other man the people of Darlington had ever seen. He was certainly a novelty to Seebohm Rowntree, the Quaker who had given him employment as his secretary and had introduced him to British politics. But whatever Seebohm Rowntree thought the future might hold for the buoyant Hungarian he could not have envisaged a British MP becoming a spy for Germany.

Even today the record is unique, but when the crunch came in 1914 Ignatius Timothy Trebitsch-Lincoln found himself able, like Sir Roger Casement,[1] to work against the best interests of a country that had treated him well and honourably. But then Trebitsch-Lincoln was a man who had small use for honour. He was a charlatan, a rogue, and a mountebank. It was almost inevitable that he became a secret agent and spy for someone, and certainly not surprising that he was for a time not only a double agent but was involved in a number of counter-espionage operations. He broke upon the European scene like a meteor. Like a meteor unable to check its own flight he passed from it. But when

---

[1] See 'A Matter of High Treason' in the author's *Stories of Famous Modern Trials* (Arthur Barker Ltd.)

he had gone he left behind an incredible story of a man whose entire life was a changing masquerade.

He was born in the small town of Paks in the Danube basin, where his father owned a yard where river-boats were built. The family were Jewish and the younger son Ignatius was intended to become a rabbi. However, a cloistered life had little appeal for a young man who learned foreign languages quickly and fluently. Ignatius Trebitsch, as the young man was known in Paks, left home when he was twenty, ostensibly to see the world, and by the time he reached London he had seen most of what Europe could offer to a young Jew's interested gaze.

In London he took the first step to divorce himself from his genuine background. He became a member of the Church of England. When he found his way back to the boatyard on the Danube his father threatened to disown him. He refused to be dismayed by his father's threats or his mother's tears. He left home for the second time and arrived in Hamburg, where he became a Lutheran. It was 1899 and he allowed himself to be recruited as a Lutheran missionary to Canada with the special task of converting Jews. Apparently his religious coat did not fit or was not comfortable, for he again transferred his beliefs and person to the Church of England, and after arriving in Germany decided he would prefer England. He persuaded his superiors to send him to the Kentish village of Appledore, but here he found himself isolated and made to feel a foreigner, which he resented. Accordingly he went to London and tried his ready hand at journalism. He was very much less than a spectacular success. But he was ready for another move in 1906, when he made the acquaintance of the noted Quaker Seebohm Rowntree, and through him received an introduction to politics, especially those of the Liberal Party.

At this time the Hungarian who could not master the slurring accent in his speech when he spoke English was a not very impressive figure. He had a face with sloping planes and forehead that was almost Asiatic, thin hair plastered tightly to his scalp, and he usually wore a pair of metal-framed pince-nez that gave him a supercilious appearance.

Four years later he had left Rowntree's employ after pocketing several hundred pounds of his employer's ready cash and forging his name to a bill to take his seat in the House of Commons, where he found little approval. Indeed, although he chose to ignore it, he knew very well that for a number of his Parliamentary colleagues he was a figure of fun. He took the occasion offered by his party to travel to Europe, ostensibly to study economic and social conditions on the Continent. He absented himself so long abroad that his travels making contacts with various politicians created suspicion as to his motives. When he returned to fight the General Election before the First World War he lost his seat. It was a case of being back to square one. Before he could make a move to better a now precarious position, with debts mounting monthly, Europe had toppled over the brink into armed conflict.

The opportunist then approached the War Office for a post as a foreign-language censor. He was given a trial which did not last long. Next he approached a department of British Intelligence with a proposal that he might be useful in planting false information where the Germans could come by it. He was given the introduction by someone he had met when an MP. When he was informed that this might not prove practicable he was ready with a scheme about decoy British naval vessels being used to entice German warships from Kiel. It was a scheme that held little prospect of success, while it would be a sure way of informing the German Naval Intelligence of the disposition of certain British capital ships.

British Intelligence decided to watch this would-be helper. Meantime a check was made on his antecedents and background. What was turned up did not inspire a great deal of confidence. In fact, Trebitsch was fortunate to remain at liberty and not to be interned as an enemy alien, for Hungary was a partner in the Central Powers bloc.

His next proposal was that he should be smuggled into Rotterdam, in neutral Holland, where he would approach the German Intelligence network and offer his services. 'I will then be able to serve the best interests of Great Britain,' he said with a show of deep sincerity, 'for I shall be able to send back vital information.'

It was glib – too glib. It sounded like a proposal from a double agent. The key men in British Intelligence debated Trebitsch and decided to try him out. 'If he comes unstuck,' said a cynical realist, 'they will have to deal with him, not us.' Arrangements were made to get him to Rotterdam, and he arrived there in December and lost little time in approaching the German consul-general in the Dutch port. He was unaware that a man who saw him call at the house with the Hohenzollern coat of arms over the front door was actually a British agent who had been alerted and was trailing the Hungarian. Indeed, it was soon apparent to British counter-spies that Trebitsch had not only been accepted by the Germans as an undercover agent, but was actively working for them. The nature of the inquiries he made indicated this.

A report was sent back to England and was passed to Sir Reginald Hall of 40 OB fame. He was chief of British Naval Intelligence. Sir Reginald asked for the first pieces of information sent back to Britain by this man who professed he wished to serve her. When they were passed to him they were carefully analysed and found to be worthless. 'The man's a fraud,' Sir Reginald told his staff. 'Possibly a dangerous one. We must get him out of Europe and somewhere where he won't be a menace.' To achieve this end Trebitsch was smuggled out of Holland and back to England where he was interviewed personally by Sir Reginald, who did not mince words. 'The only way you can serve this country,' Trebitsch was told bluntly, 'is to get out of it and stay out – the farther the better.'

The alternative was not stressed because there was no need. The shifty Hungarian knew the score. If he refused to leave England he would be interned. He bought a single ticket to New York on the SS *Philadelphia* and stepped ashore in the United States on 9 February. Not many hours later he found a way of presenting himself to a German agent, who related what he had been told to his chiefs. But the Germans thought he had been planted by the British, an idea that had not been omitted from Sir Reginald Hall's shrewd calculations, and they refused to commit themselves, instead playing delaying tactics in order to gain time to test the newcomer.

Trebitsch meanwhile presented himself at several offices and met editors of pro-German journals. He was still working to impress German Intelligence with his *bona fides* as a useful German agent when the bill he had forged in the name of Seebohm Rowntree was discovered and reported to the police. In consequence the American Government was approached to approve the extradition to Britain of the. wanted forger to stand trial. Because it was wartime and Trebitsch was a Hungarian national in a neutral country the processes that led to eventual agreement took time. It was on 4 August, the first anniversary of Great Britain declaring war on Germany, that Trebitsch was arrested, the charge read to him, and he was escorted to a ship returning to England.

At his trial he was found guilty and sentenced to be imprisoned. He was released four years later, in the summer of 1919. By that time not only was the war in Europe over, but a good many changes had come to the post-war Continent, including Hungary, where the Communist leader Bela Kun sat passing out death sentences in Budapest. When Trebitsch heard that he was to be deported it was like a sentence of death to the man so recently freed.

However, by some amazing power of resiliency he arrived in Budapest and survived the purge being made by the militant followers of Bela Kun. But he wisely did not tarry when he realized his return was not welcome. He avoided arrest and reached Germany. Again he sought employment as an undercover agent by attempting to make personal contact with the former German Emperor, now interned in Holland. Although he failed he made contact with several Right Wing monarchists who said he would be a useful man for their party in Berlin.

After arriving in the German capital, Trebitsch was interviewed by a man who was preparing a *coup d'état*. He was found visible employment on the staff of a reactionary journal and worked secretly as a spy for the party organizers. When the signal was given for Kapp's rising Trebitsch was so deeply involved that he could not fully cover his tracks when the *coup d'état* failed, and fled to Munich to avoid arrest. His energies were unfailing and great effort never apparently caused him to flag. He proved this by arranging secret meetings with Herr Pohner, the Munich Chief of Police, and with the Bavarian Prime Minister, Herr Kahr. He showed them papers, undoubtedly faked, that proved the new monarchist movement had suffered only a temporary setback. Both agreed to join the movement and ensure that Bavaria put pressure on Saxony to line up with them. At the same time Mecklenburg was to bring similar political pressure on Berlin.

Indeed, Pohner provided Trebitsch, in his new role of undercover agent, with a bogus passport and cash to make journeys to Berlin, where he succeeded in being received by Ludendorff, the German general who had folded up the Russian front during the war as though it were a damp blanket. Pohner had warned the undercover agent to be on his guard against the plain-clothes men of the Berlin police. 'They have your name and they'll be looking for you,' he told Trebitsch. 'If they arrest you the passport won't fool them.'

It was another member of the monarchist movement, Captain Pabst, whose acquaintance Trebitsch had made before the abortive *Putsch* by Kapp, who took him to Ludendorff's secret hideout in the city, only to find that the general had changed his place of residence to avoid being taken prisoner by a Left Wing faction. They had to make a journey to an isolated house in the middle of a large forest near Rosenhain where they found Ludendorff looking far from well, and he did not take a major part in the discussion that ensued between Trebitsch and Captain Pabst on the one hand and Major Stephani on the other. The secret meeting ended with grudging agreement that Trebitsch's plan should be followed and the headquarters of the movement transferred to Hungary, so that overtures could be made to both the Austrian and Hungarian Royalist factions, with a view to settling on Vienna as eventual headquarters for a united monarchist movement.

Trebitsch was now at the very heart of a secret organization depending on a spy network that was working to change the course of post-war European history. He had enjoyed a run of incredible luck since being deported from Britain, but he was chancing his arm when he returned to Berlin to attend a monarchist conference in May. He was told not to spend the night in Berlin because the Criminal Police were on the lookout for him. So he went to Trebbin, near Potsdam, and stayed the night in the home of a governess whom he knew. The next morning he was waiting for the Berlin train to arrive at the local station when he was recognized by a detective of the Criminal Police and arrested. But the prisoner's presence of mind did not forsake him. 'Before we leave let me collect some of my things,' he requested, and was taken back to the room where he had spent the night. Instead of packing a bag he escaped through the window. When the hunt recommenced he was hidden in the house of someone whose name was on a list of supporters of the movement. He returned to Munich by way of Frankfurt. However, by this time all German police forces had been alerted to be on the lookout for the chief secret agent and spy of the monarchist movement. Trebitsch was only able to evade them because Police Chief Pohner had written to the Hungarian consul-general in Munich a personal recommendation for aid.

Trebitsch was given a guard in the person of a Hungarian junior consul, who accompanied him to Vienna. But the Austrian police had been alerted in turn. The secret emissary had to find a refuge in a hurry. Again he risked a big bluff, this time by approaching the Hungarian Ambassador direct for assistance. The ambassador had a new passport made out for his visitor and explained that a new Government was running the country since the fall of Bela Kun. Trebitsch was given the names of two Hungarian deputies who might be considered sympathetic to the monarchist cause and a letter to Colonel von Pronay, the Government's Chief Press Officer.

Within a few days Trebitsch was again attempting to weave his spell of espionage fantasy in order to be accepted and to become *persona grata*. He was listened to with deep attention as he detailed a scheme whereby German soldiers dressed as civilians should be allowed into the country, and then, once more in uniform, turned against both Czechoslovakia and the Austrian capital. A Colonel Vauer who attended this meeting had actually been empowered to speak on behalf of Ludendorff of a treaty signed between the monarchists and Hungary. It was the realist press agent who poured a cold douche on the scheme: 'It could only end in disaster,' he maintained. 'I could not advise supporting such a venture.' With those words he ended part of the incredible masquerade that was the life of the man who had from somewhere or nowhere found the name Lincoln which he had attached to Trebitsch.

Realizing that his bolt in that part of the continent had been shot into the blue and had landed ineffectively far from the intended target, the poseur and fast-talking agent of the monarchist leaders, who were reluctant to gamble on success, left that secret meeting and turned his back on the Nordics, so many of whom had proved unfriendly to a man with his cast of countenance. He was of a mind to go south.

As he crossed into Italy, it was as though a curtain fell behind him as he continued south over the Brenner Pass. No one has been able to discover the moves he made, the contacts he sought, or what he offered as inducements to those who listened to him. But before long he was again involved with underground workers, this time of the Fascist movement, and it is certain that he was accepted by the Fascists as a useful spy and contact with the world north of the Brenner. What is far less certain is that he was concerned in the conspiracy that ended with the assassination of the Socialist deputy Giacomo Matteotti in 1924, though that claim has been made. He may have known of the conspiracy, but the chances of his having taken any active part in the murder in a car in broad daylight are exceedingly remote. That was an essentially Italian crime, performed by Mussolini's toadies to remove a man who was an embarrassment to their leader. Besides, the role of spy fitted Trebitsch snugly. He thrived on intrigues and double-dealing. He was a great believer in bluff to serve his ends because he could rely on his own fast tongue. Violence was foreign to his nature. Untrained in the use of firearms and poor of sight, he was only a man of action when in the shadows.

While Trebitsch was in Italy the shadows were rather crowded, for Mussolini had a veritable army of secret agents working for him, and it is possible that if Trebitsch was used at all it was only when covered by other agents. This could explain why there is no record of him arriving again in his earlier field of operation and trying to evolve some fresh snare for the inept who had grandiose notions about their political worthiness. Indeed, it was in Italy that mystery began to surround the person of the furtive charlatan. When he disappeared from Europe is not known. However, it is reasonably certain that when he finally left the Continent it was from an Italian port that he sailed. And his general direction was east, for the next surprising report of his activities came from China, where yet another religion and a further role encouraged him to start upon still stranger secret adventures. For what ultimate purpose? The answer seems to be so that he could become an effective spy for the Japanese.

Indeed, Ignatius Trebitsch, the Hungarian Jew who had been in turn a Lutheran missionary, Church of England curate, British Member of Parliament, double agent, confessed German spy and Right Wing subversive as well as a Fascist, had climaxed his amazing career by becoming a Buddhist monk in order to facilitate his work as a spy. He had already lived a career that had made him world news. But now the rather full dark moustache was gone, as was the hair parted in the middle, the starched wing collars, and the pince-nez. A new picture appeared in the world's newspapers. It showed Trebitsch as a gowned monk in yellow fustian, with shaven head and two rows of prayer beads looped around his neck. Wrinkles were etched at the sides of his mouth. He posed with his right hand folded over his left, gaze direct and slightly challenging, as though he no longer needed glasses to correct myopia. Reports appeared claiming that this Buddhist monk was an abbot named Chao Kung, who was a political adviser to Wu Pei-fu, but a close scrutiny revealed more of a European than an Oriental in the face above the yellow gown. Journalists who scented a good story went out of their way to meet the abbot, but they did not find him. Instead, the abbot himself walked into the offices of the *Strait Times* and in carefully enunciated English requested the newspaper files so that he could look through them. He was handed the section he asked for and while he was reading a journalist who had known him in Europe came up and stood waiting for him to stop reading.

When the man in the saffron robe looked up quizzically the journalist inquired:

'Aren't you Trebitsch-Lincoln?'
'I am the Abbot Chao Kung,' said the monk.
The journalist would not be put off. 'But you used to be Trebitsch-Lincoln,' he persisted.
The monk sat very still, hands crossed on the newspaper file. 'The past is past,' he said in a toneless voice. 'I am the Abbot Chao Kung.'
'Why are you consulting the back issues?' he was asked.
'I am about to go to Europe.'

It was hardly an explanation until one learned more about Trebitsch's family life. At some time he had married a European woman and she bore him three sons. One of these, John Lincoln, became a soldier in the British Army. In 1926 he was arrested and charged with the murder of a brewers' salesman named Edward Richards. The jury found him guilty and he was sentenced to death. The Abbot Chao Kung was about to revert to the man he had been, Ignatius Timothy Trebitsch-Lincoln, and to return to Europe to see his unhappy son before the man's execution. He sailed from Colombo to reach England by an indirect route. Such a choice of travel was a mistake. He was still on the Continent on the morning John Lincoln was hanged. He did not return to Ceylon, which was where he had first donned the saffron robe and taken on a fresh personality. Instead, he journeyed to Shanghai and reverted to the role of a Buddhist monk. Posing again as an abbot he acquired as followers three other

62

Buddhist monks and six Buddhist nuns, whom he described as his companions for peace.

There is little doubt today, however, that this peaceful role was no more than effective camouflage that allowed him to act as an active agent for the Japanese. For a year he procured and passed on to Japanese contacts a wealth of valuable information to any enemy of the Chinese. The facts and figures passed on to them by the Hungarian now masquerading as an Oriental unquestionably helped the Japanese when they threw off all pretence and attacked China in 1937. It also proved the time for the Abbot Chao Kung to doff pretence. He openly declared his allegiance to the hereditary enemy the Chinese had referred to forty years before as the Shrimp People. Indeed, some of the incensed Chinese claimed he had been not only a spy, but had also been an active Fifth Columnist in the pay of his Japanese employers.

Although despised and hated by the Chinese, the bogus abbot unquestionably performed ably in the sight of the Japanese and presumably was paid amply for his services. Indeed, he was still working for them when, a couple of years later, the Second World War opened in Europe. This time the professional spy ready to sell his services where they would bring the highest profit went to Tibet, where his employers supplied him with a radio station. When its locality was discovered by counter-spies it was left still broadcasting propaganda, but Trebitsch moved on to another station and began a fresh round of propaganda. Each time the station he used was located he went on to another, harder to locate, until eventually there was a chain of radio stations spilling Axis propaganda into the Oriental ether. The man responsible for the programmes and the times they went on the air was Trebitsch-Lincoln, still playing the role that gave him most pleasure – the spy with power to be actively subversive.

Not that he did not find time to embellish his incredible masquerade with some almost unbelievably audacious refinements. In April 1939 for instance, five months before the declaration of war after German troops had invaded

Poland, he wrote a letter to the Pope, which amounted to an appeal for His Holiness to rouse himself personally and head a crusade for peace 'founded on true Christianity,' as the charlatan had the gall to pen.

Failing to obtain any reaction that he could consider satisfactory, he next produced his own plan for peace. Again the man in a Buddhist gown, who had been born a Jew and in his time had been several shades of Christian, was apparently obsessed with the eventual fate of Christianity. He wrote to the newspapers in Shanghai, announcing that he had produced a plan for, in his own words, 'a last attempt to save the Christian world,' and went on to invite all world leaders and figureheads except Stalin to meet him. It was outlandish posing. It probably amused the Japanese as bold effrontery by a skilled propagandist. But was it something more? Was the spy who knew so much really giving something away? It is at least interesting to speculate.

His announcements in the Shanghai Press appeared in February 1941. That is, four months before Hitler drove eastwards into Russia, which had a brilliant spy in Japan named Richard Sorge who was feeding back valuable information to the Kremlin. Sorge is generally believed to have known Hitler's intentions against the Soviet. Did the Japanese know what Sorge knew, and had Trebitsch-Lincoln acquired the same knowledge from a secret source? It is not impossible. Moreover, Japan was preparing to jump the United States fleet in Pearl Harbour when assured that the Nazis had the upper hand east of Poland. It would be not unlikely that Trebitsch-Lincoln, working for the Japanese and preparing their Far East propaganda broadcasts, had at least warning of such an attack being a possibility. If that attack was made, he knew, the result would be a grim confrontation between the Anglo-American forces and those of their allies opposed to the forces of the Axis Powers. Did he secretly believe there could be only one outcome to such an Armageddon? Did he, one man, and with his tongue in his cheek at that, try to write a warning that was both obscure and preposterous?

To know the character of Trebitsch-Lincoln is to know

that the man was capable of any quirk or twist of deceit, and that he was seldom able to find his life and purpose so rewarding as when he was engaged in playing one group off against another. For he was a man who, primarily, had a built-in inferiority complex that had to be compensated by acts which demonstrated he was, through artifice and chicanery, the superior of those he sought to delude and cheat. This was a terribly dangerous characteristic in a spy. But Trebitsch-Lincoln was also a supreme confidence trickster, and in his fashion a brilliant liar.

For instance, during that period when he had absented himself on the Continent and was seldom seen in his seat in the House of Commons he was not just making contacts, valuable as some of these were to prove later when he became a German monarchist agent. He was for a while in Rumania, forming a syndicate to purchase oil rights to some of the wells in the Ploesti oilfield. His glibness enabled him to use the money of other members of the syndicate to make eighteen thousand pounds for himself. By any standard this was the work of a very smart operator. Moreover, he did not bring the money back to England. It was left where it would be of use to him when he found it necessary to recross the English Channel and keep travelling south.

Not surprisingly Trebitsch avoided being brought to retribution after the defeat of the Axis Powers, but only by dying twenty months after announcing his Christian peace plan to the Shanghai newspapers. He died on 7 October 1943, and was buried in his yellow robe as the Buddhist Abbot Chao Kung. His deserted widow survived him for sixteen years. She died in London in 1959.

6 They Called Her Tiger Eyes

A few days after the first shots had been fired in the First World War, in August 1914, the Chief of Intelligence of the German General Staff, Colonel Walther Nicolai, received a letter posted in Freiburg, in the Black Forest. It was from someone named Schragmüller who claimed to have a fluent command and knowledge of English, Italian, and French and to be engaged in post-graduate research at the local university. 'I should like a post with our troops at the front, where my services might be of value,' the writer explained somewhat naïvely. The busy colonel tossed the letter in a tray to be filed away and conveniently lost. He then proceded to forget Schragmüller, which did not prove difficult.

However, a few days later he received another letter from Schragmüller, reminding him of the first and of the offer contained in it.

'Damn the man,' Colonel Nicolai growled to his secretary. 'Here, put this with the other,' and passed over the letter for filing with the first. He did not reply to either.

But the unknown but persistent Schragmüller was not to be put off by silence from performing a patriotic duty. Other letters continued to arrive at the colonel's office, until he felt something should be done to stop their flow. Schragmüller was becoming a nuisance. He said to his secretary, 'Arrange for the Civil Censorship Bureau in Brussels to give Schragmüller a post with them. That should get the damned fellow off my back and give him something useful to do.'

In this way a Lieutenant Schragmüller became appointed to the Censorship Bureau in Brussels, which had been taken by the advancing German forces and was under the control of a harsh governor-general named von Bissing, who was later to ensure that the English nurse Edith Cavell was executed.[1]

For a couple of weeks the newly appointed Lieutenant Schragmüller worked efficiently in an office of the bureau, and then suggestions began to come from that office in the lieutenant's handwriting. The notes dealt with Intelligence matters deriving from the lieutenant's work. They were passed on to the Intelligence staff attached to the army commanded by General von Beseler, which was investing Antwerp. It was not long before the general was asking questions and was informed of the voluntary Intelligence work undertaken by a lieutenant attached to the Brussels Censorship Bureau. 'He seems to know what to look for', von Beseler told his chief aide. 'Send for him and fix a time for me to see him.'

If the receipt of a summons to attend the general provided the lieutenant with an unexpected surprise, it was not to be measured against the surprise received by General von Beseler when the lieutenant entered his campaign headquarters and saluted. For the lieutenant did not wear trousers, but a skirt. 'Good God!' the general exclaimed. 'There's been a mistake.' The lieutenant smiled. It was a truly lovely feminine smile surrounded by a grey uniform with collar badges and a shiny-peaked military cap set squarely on lovely blonde hair built up tidily at the nape of the neck. 'No mistake, General,' announced this amazing phenomenon. 'I am Lieutenant Elsbeth Schragmüller, reporting as instructed.'

Some minutes later General von Beseler was a very enlightened field commander. Not only had he proved to himself that Fräulein Dr Lieutenant Elsbeth Schragmüller had a sharp mind and a natural instinct for Intelligence matters, but that she was a person of some academic distinction. The daughter of a sound middle-class family in

<hr>

[1]See 'The White Lady and Others' in the author's *Stories of Famous Spies* (Arthur Barker Ltd.)

Westphalia, she had obtained her doctorate at Freiburg University in 1913 with a philosophic treatise on the ancient German craft guilds entitled *Die Bruderschaft der Borer und Balierer von Freiburg und Waldkirch.* The general was sufficiently perceptive as a man to realize that in feminine clothes the blue-eyed blonde lieutenant, who was in her mid-twenties, would be an extremely attractive woman. In uniform she performed like a man, attentive to detail, able to concentrate, and sharp to reach a justifiable conclusion. He sent for one of his Intelligence Staff officers, Captain Refer, and enjoyed the captain's frank shock at being introduced to a woman in uniform. 'Captain,' said von Beseler, 'I want you to evaluate for me some conclusions arrived at by Lieutenant Schragmüller from letters censored in Brussels.'

It was Captain Refer's turn to be surprised by the work undertaken by the *Fräulein* in Brussels and the penetrating conclusions she had drawn. 'Well?' snapped the general. The captain realized that von Beseler had already made up his mind to have this amazing young woman working for him, but that the general wanted the overt suggestion to come from someone attached to Intelligence. He said, 'Lieutenant Schragmüller would, in my opinion, General, be better employed with our Special Intelligence Corps.' 'That's what I think,' the general approved.

Elsbeth Schragmüller was accordingly sent back to Brussels to await a fresh posting. This was not delayed, and within a matter of days she found herself returning to Germany and making for Baden-Baden under orders to report to Major Joseph Salonek of the Nachrichtendienst, who was in charge of the largest of three establishments for the training of Military Intelligence officers and secret agents. Here the *Fräulein* lieutenant surrendered her rank and name and even her sex and became a mere number. She kept strict hours, was allowed only a small sum regularly as pocket money, and was billeted in some back-street lodgings. She was trained to become a person capable of being a complete nonentity and merging with her immediate background in such a way that she would draw no attention to herself.

Precisely at eight each morning she was in a classroom,

ready to begin lessons. These ranged widely in subjects. She was taught how to read and draw a map and to draw a detailed plan of a building or a district in a town with different kinds of buildings. For hours she studied army insignia of all kinds, and the various ranks these represented. She became conversant with the military uniforms of a dozen different countries. She studied the basics of military security and even the methods of detectives in civilian police forces. She was taught how to interview suspects and hesitant friends alike, how to enable the former to trick themselves, how first to find reason for suspicion, and how to evaluate coded messages. She experimented with invisible inks, underwent tests for discovering them, and even learned how to manufacture them.

From the time of her arrival in morning class until she finished her classwork some time after five in the afternoon Fräulein Schragmüller wore a mask over the upper half of her face. This face mask was *de rigueur* for all pupils of the Intelligence school. It was used more for its psychological value than for any practical purpose, as was the routine for their leaving each day – at three-minute intervals and singly, and in the knowledge that each would be followed to his or her lodging by a plain-clothes man. Off-duty times were also occasions for detectives to be watching the pupils of Major Salonek.

It was a grim and testing time for all pupils, and not surprisingly a fair number failed the passing-out examinations. But not Fräulein Schragmüller. She received very high marks, and looked forward to being smuggled abroad and given a task in an enemy country. She was sent for by Major Salonek, who shocked her by letting her into a secret. She had not been trained in Baden-Baden to be an active spy in an enemy country. She had been put through the customary spy-training course so that she could be observed, how she worked, what progress she made, and how she reacted to the routine. Also, how she performed in the passing-out examinations. 'You have done excellently. You are too ·good material to be lost in field work,' the major told her. 'You are to train others. You are being sent to Antwerp, where a new espionage school is being opened. You are being promoted, and will shortly be joining the teaching staff.'

Elsbeth Schragmüller was keenly disappointed, but she did not allow herself to appear let-down by the decision that had been taken. 'I shall do my best, Major.' It was her usual attitude. She would do her best. But the words were not merely conventional assurance when spoken by her. They amounted to a solemn promise, for that was her nature.

Some days later she arrived at the Belgium corner house where the Rue de l'Harmonie met the Rue de la Pépinière. It had an entrance in each street and was under the direction of Major Groos, an Intelligence officer with a splendid reputation in the Service. His staff were all picked personnel. Indeed, the Nachrichtendienst had been combed thoroughly to provide the major's staff. They were all men except Elsbeth Schragmüller, who, as a woman, was something in the nature of an experiment. Most of the males who were her staff companions and colleagues thought the idea of using a woman as an Intelligence teacher was a poor joke that was not genuinely diverting. Before many weeks she changed the minds of all in the establishment. She proved herself better at her teaching work than any other member of the staff. She even found fault with some of the school's methods and justified her findings. She became feared by some of the less competent staff members. A few tried to reach her by over-tures of friendship. They failed. Others invited her out to dinner, hoping to advance from her acceptance. She courteously refused all such offers. She remained aloof, became involved in no essentially masculine rivalries. In effect, she was untouchable. She became the most successful teacher in the establishment and before very long a legend grew up about her among the Allied Intelligence Services.

It was claimed that at the school she was known behind her back as Tiger Eyes, because nothing missed her gaze and it was merciless in discovering flaws. But she turned out some exceptionally well-trained spies. It was said later that even the notorious Mata Hari[1] was sent by the Germans to attend

[1] See 'The White Lady and Others' in the author's *Stories of Famous Spies* (Arthur Barker Ltd.)

her specially designed refresher courses, in which trained and experienced spies were taught the latest techniques and brought up to date with the kind of counter-spies who were operating to uncover their work.

Fräulein Schragmüller earned a nickname among the Allied Staffs in Europe. She was 'the Beautiful Blonde of Antwerp' to them although none of them had seen her or even a picture of her. It was believed that the work she was doing was indirectly responsible for more German success, militarily and diplomatically, than anyone could gauge. British Intelligence tried desperately with their own agents in Belgium and Holland to pierce the identity of the blonde in Antwerp whom the French were beginning to label 'Mademoiselle Docteur.' They had no success, for Elsbeth Schragmüller refused to have her photograph taken or to give interviews to a German journalist, even when he had military permission to approach her. If she refused to give an interview it was useless for the journalist to attempt to go over her head and have her superiors give her a direct order to comply with the request. She was invariably backed up in her decisions by those who had grown to have implicit trust in her judgement at all levels.

French agents seeking to discover the real identity of Mademoiselle Docteur had no more success than the British. She existed: that was all that was known for certain by the Allies. But they suffered from new espionage techniques she invented for agents in the field. Chief among these was the one that came to be referred to in the Antwerp school as 'the Sacrifice'. This meant that an agent was deliberately chosen as an espionage scapegoat and was sacrificed by being allowed to betray himself or herself in order that the heat could be taken off a more valuable agent who was performing much more vital work. One agent, in short, was sacrificed to save another or to keep intact a more important agent's identity or contacts. This became a technique that was particularly irksome to the French, who were at times forced to arrest the person they didn't want while the one they sought and wanted very badly stayed effectively concealed or managed to escape to a fresh hideout.

Developing from the invention or improvement of a technique was the general overseeing of an agent's career, and this is something else Tiger Eyes – incidentally they were a bright and penetrating pale blue – is believed to have innovated. This was quite apart from the direction afforded by a superior agent or spymaster directing a number of active agents. There is scope for believing that Mati Hari not only attended the Antwerp school, but was evaluated as a high risk by Elsbeth Schragmüller, who later recommended that she be tossed to the French when she had become a danger because she had been playing the role of double agent, which was discovered by Mademoiselle Docteur.

The agents who passed through her hands for grooming and preparing for fieldwork gave up fifteen weeks to learning what she had to teach them. She made sure that it was a gruelling process for them, for she was pitiless in testing the quality of the human material she had to make over into professional spies who could perform without risk to those directing their operations.

Her embryo agents lived at 10 Rue de la Pépinière, which was enclosed by a brickwalled courtyard, and all windows facing the street were shuttered. They did not wear domino masks, but for the first three weeks when they retired to their rooms they were locked in. On the outside of the door was hung a card with the occupant's printed code name. He ate, slept, and did his training in that room, visited by the blonde with hard eyes. For those three weeks he did not take outside exercise. When he did he walked around in the courtyard – alone. In many respects the burgeoning spy was a prisoner and was made to feel he was. It was all part of the intended psychological adjustment to what, three months later, might become suddenly a harsh reality.

Tiger Eyes concentrated on two special aspects of making successful spies – morale and security. She believed the one followed the other in natural sequence, and she was time and again proved right. She remained dedicated to the work of her incredible spy factory until the end of hostilities in 1918, when she returned to Germany with the defeated German armies, a woman to whom it had all suddenly been in vain.

There had been days when she had spent twenty hours of the twenty-four at her post. There had even been days when she had given orders, so it is believed, for the elimination of poor material that had learned too much about her work and methods. She wished to avoid receiving any personal publicity that might help the enemy.

For Fräulein Schragmüller defeat was hard to accept. It was a reversal of all dreams and hopes and even calculated assessments. She chose to vanish into obscurity. She did not write her memoirs, which would have been some of the most interesting about the development of the German espionage system. Indeed nothing was heard of her for more than a decade, and it was not until a German-speaking woman was accepted as a patient in a Swiss sanatorium during the 1930s that the legend of Tiger Eyes was revived. Someone discovered that the woman in the sanatorium had been a German secret agent during the recent war. Reporters arrived and made inquiries, and before long the story was in world-wide circulation that the sick woman was Elsbeth Schragmüller, who had been admitted after becoming a drug addict.

This was sensational, but was untrue, and the patient's reaction was impulsive, almost completely out of character with what was known of the ice-cold Tiger Eyes of the war years. She gave a press interview and admitted that she was Elsbeth Schragmüller, but the drug-taking story was a vicious lie. She claimed that after the close of hostilities she had returned to academic work and had been a lecturer at Munich University but not taking any part in the general social life of the city. She had lived alone with her mother until her health had broken down.

Speculation died, for she had shown that she was still capable of dealing with a personal emergency, but the legend remained and continued after her death a few years later when another war had broken out upon the world stage. She did nothing that is known to help Hitler attempt to succeed where the Hohenzollerns had failed. Even for Elsbeth Schragmüller the Beautiful Blonde of Antwerp and Mademoiselle Docteur had become only names with no lingering reality beyond already fading memories.

The substance of the legend her activities had created, however, outlasted her in a curious quality of grudging fame. For instance, there were quite a few Allied Intelligence officers who in 1918 firmly believed that the Antwerp blonde was also the spy known as Maria de Victorica, whose trail was first discovered by British agents in 1914 and shortly afterwards by the French. The trail was lost, which was certainly what one would expect of Tiger Eyes. But it was picked up again in November 1917 after British Intelligence sent a coded message to Washington, alerting the Americans that a German blonde female agent had secretly left Madrid for New York with ten thousand US dollars. The Federal agents were provided by the British with two likely addresses, but these were found to be deserted. However, both were watched, and early in the New Year a letter addressed to one of the addresses was stopped and examined. Invisible writing in a known German secret ink listed as F type produced a fresh address, a boarding-house where a steward on a ship recently arrived from Europe normally stayed.

The man was picked up and questioned and claimed he had been given two letters to post so that they would have American postmarks. Shortly after he had agreed to post the letters his ship sailed. He professed to know nothing of the letters' contents, but the one which had been stopped had directives in the secret writing about the destruction of American munitions factories. That letter had been addressed to a woman. American agents called at another address the steward had posted letters to, but were confronted by an elderly woman who claimed to have a poor memory but eventually recalled a name. It was Victorica.

When the Americans asked the British if they knew the name it was to be told they did indeed. So did the French, who had actually arrested a man they believed to be a spy who was married to her. The description London had of Victorica fitted a woman of that name who was passed through immigration around the end of 1916 to a liner sailing for New York. She had an Argentine passport. In the

United States a great search began to find this woman, now believed to be a top German agent who had come from Antwerp. So it was not long before the theory was formulated that this was the Beautiful Blonde of Antwerp undertaking a special field mission.

The hunt for her became intense. Every hotel and boarding house in the New York area was checked by American detectives or undercover agents. One lead was produced when it was learned that she had registered at the Waldorf Astoria and paid in advance for several months. She had stayed only a short while. What was even more puzzling was that this strange procedure was found to have been duplicated when the same woman had booked in at the Spencer Arms. She seemed to have plenty of funds. However, after leaving the Spencer Arms quite suddenly her trail gave out. She had vanished, and the Americans had arrived at a dead end.

It was from London again that the next lead came. The Intelligence files had supplied the British searchers with the name of a German firm in New York that was suspected by the British of having been set up with considerable cash reserves solely to act as bankers for active German agents in the USA. The British suggested the Americans check whether Maria de Victorica had drawn funds from that firm, which was still operating under a legitimate front.

It was not long before the Americans were satisfied that a blonde woman, very good-looking, and in her mid-thirties, had drawn the considerable sum of thirty-five thousand dollars from the firm's reserves. They wanted the woman's address. 'It is only a temporary one,' they were informed, but the address was another dead end, at least until they checked with a foreign mission, where some uncollected letters for her had been left to await her return. These were confiscated, and back in Washington the scientists went to work on them. Again invisible inks were brought out and the messages between innocent-seeming lines of ordinary ink read. What the Americans had stumbled on, almost literally, shocked them.

Maria de Victorica had been concerned with passing to

other parties plans for widening sabotage activities which had possibly emanated from a house on the corner of the Rue de la Pépinière in Brussels. Moreover, Victorica was implicated in a scheme to land German U-boats in the Mexican Gulf to put ashore supplies of tetra, known to be the most destructive explosive produced to that date by German scientists. There were the names of known and suspected professional saboteurs secreted between the ordinary lines of those letters, including 'Dynamite Charlie' Wunnenberg.

The value of those recovered letters became even greater when it was found that she was ordering church statuary from manufacturers in Zürich. A number of Catholic priests would be helping her to get the statues through the American and Swiss customs. By this time the American Intelligence agents, very thoroughly awake and considerably perturbed, had little doubt what would eventually be packed into the hollow spaces of the statues, just as they were certain that the statues, stuffed with tetra, would be left in buildings far more industrially vital than churches.

But the real and paramount problem remained – where was this incredibly dangerous undercover agent? The order was given to put under active surveillance anyone known to have seen the woman or had dealings with her, however innocently, and at the same time to investigate every name found in her correspondence, even those in the ordinary letter written in clear.

If the Americans had been less than thorough they would have missed a vital clue. Fortunately they did not. A cousin of an innocent-seeming name was a regular attendant at St Patrick's Cathedral in New York City. She made a point of entering the cathedral daily and always at the same time, fifteen minutes past the hour. An agent followed her inside when she was carrying a folded newspaper under her arm. She entered the same pew she had been choosing regularly. This time she left the newspaper when she rose to her feet and walked out. She was going through the entrance when an elderly man entered the pew she had left. He too was carrying a newspaper under his arm. When he rose to leave he still had a newspaper under his arm, but it was the one the woman had left.

The elderly man was followed to Pennsylvania Station and a Federal agent was with him when he took a train to Long Island. He left the train at Long Beach, still followed, and took a taxi to the Nassau Hotel. Another taxi that drew up at the hotel carried the agent. He followed the elderly man into the hotel lounge and sat across from him when he sat smoking and looking through his newspaper. When the elderly man rose leisurely he left his newspaper on a bench seat. Before the agent could move to recover it a smartly dressed woman carrying a collection of newspapers took the seat the elderly man had vacated. She spread her newspapers about on the bench seat and settled apparently to enjoy perusing them.

There was something familiar about her. After racking his brain the agent realized this woman fitted the known and memorized description of the wanted Maria de Victorica. He hurried to a phone. The arrest of the smart woman who liked reading newspapers was almost routine. But she was found to have an unknown name. It was Marie de Vussier, not a very impressive *nom-de-guerre*, as it relied upon actual initials. Of course she denied that she was anyone other than who she claimed to be, and she had plenty of paperwork to back that up. But she became silent when a laboratory in Washington distilled from her silk scarves, found in her hotel room, enough of the F type secret ink to enable her to continue writing invisible messages for many months. There was even a stylo-type pen that was constructed to keep the secret ink flow even.

When she was told she broke down, and her collapse was complete. She had to be sent to a hospital where she was guarded day and night and kept incommunicado. She was too weak to be brought to trial. When she died the Americans had no way of assessing the number of espionage secrets she had not shared. She was buried in Westchester County under the name of Hawthorne.

It was almost inevitable that the woman who died in the prison ward of Bellevue Hospital in New York on 12 August

1920, after a wasting illness lasting two years which physicians were powerless to combat, should be identified by some of her former adversaries in espionage as Elsbeth Schragmüller, but she was older, and was much more likely to be Maria von Kretschman, a first-line spy working under direct orders from Colonel Walther Nicolai, the man who first found a job for Tiger Eyes, and the daughter of Baron Hans von Kretschman, a political historian.

What is certainly true is that she had gone through one of Elsbeth Schragmüller's refresher courses at one time, and her end might have come when she was acting out a typical piece of espionage work designed by the Beautiful Blonde of Antwerp, whose legendary image she blurred more than three thousand miles from that Belgian city, but quite unintentionally. It has been stated categorically that the records of the US Corps of Intelligence Police still refer to the woman who died in Bellevue, New York City, as the 'Beautiful Blonde Woman of Antwerp'. But while she might have been a Beautiful Blonde Woman *from* Antwerp, she was not the notorious Mademoiselle Docteur and no one had ever called the lovely blonde noblewoman Tiger Eyes.

7 A Scot Who Liked Puzzles

About the time Admiral Hall, Chief of British Naval Intelligence at the outbreak of hostilities in 1914, was deciding Ignatius Timothy Trebitsch-Lincoln was poor material for use by his department, he was having very different thoughts about a Scots professor, who seemed to him just the man Naval Intelligence required if it were to break German naval codes.

Professor Alfred Ewing travelled south to attend a meeting in London. It was put to him that he might better serve the country by directing the setting-up of a cipher-breaking bureau. Ewing had a tidy mind that revelled in mathematics and acrostic puzzles. He enjoyed the more profound type of crossword puzzle and any mechanical problem erected on a basis of figures.

'You'll have your own staff,' he was promised, 'and you can pick them yourself.'

'No strings?' the Scot asked the naval man.

'Not any that will be knotted by me,' was the reply. 'That good enough for you?'

'Amply.'

It wasn't a very long meeting, for both the naval officer and the Scots professor seemed to recognize qualities in the other of which he approved. Ewing agreed to set up his own coterie of experts to help him in the very necessary task of breaking enemy codes.

'By the way,' he said to Hall before leaving after formalities had been concluded, 'what particular branch of Naval Intelligence is this?'

The naval man looked blank for a moment and then grinned.

'I call us 40 OB,' he said. 'I think that's something that will puzzle any enemy agent who picks it up.'

'It sounds simple but profound,' said the Scot who enjoyed few things better than tackling puzzles.

Admiral Hall's grin spread.

'It's certainly simple,' he agreed, 'but there's nothing profound about it. This room is number forty in the Old Building of the Admiralty, so I think of us as 40 OB.'

For a moment the professor looked shocked. Then the pair of them were laughing at a joke shared.

'It might prove too profound for the Teutonic mind,' he told Hall.

'Well, let's hope so.'

Until the end of the war the Germans tried in many ways to 'crack' the mystery of that to them enigmatic 40 OB. They did not succeed. They came to accept the two figures and two letters of the term as a typical piece of British cunning in concealing the intricate with the seeming simple, a characteristic of their foes that they always distrusted, even when suspicion was not merited, as in this case.

Ewing lost no time in settling down to work in the rather bare room in the Admiralty's Old Building, which had been supplied with a safe but little to be locked in it. The staff Ewing encouraged to come to London from their university posts and to work with him soon filled the office, but had no time to stare at their rather dismal immediate surroundings. A British ship had already crept to a rendezvous point off the Dutch border with Belgium under cover of darkness and severed the marine telegraphic cables that were Germany's most secret as well as most immediate connection with the world beyond the North Sea. The ship reached England later with a good piece of German cable wound around a drum. The ends of the severed cable were left lying on the bed of the North Sea a fair distance from each other. If the Germans wanted to send any message a great distance fast they would have to resort to radio transmission. The use of codes was essential.

To transmit their coded messages the Germans had erected a powerful radio transmitting station at Nauen, in the Berlin district. It was not long before British monitoring stations were picking up German coded messages. They were sent to Naval Intelligence and found themselves on Ewing's desk in 40 OB. It was still August 1914 when Ewing and his staff were called upon to work late. The alarm was rung in London when on the 26th, a day more than three weeks after the declaration of war by Britain, a German light cruiser ran aground in the Baltic during a sudden fog. Jagged rocks holed her, and her fate was sealed when the Baltic waves began to pound her buckled hull. She had been engaged in mine-laying and destroying lighthouses that could be landmarks in navigation for enemy vessels, especially Russian from Petrograd, as St Petersburg had then been renamed.

As the ill-fated *Magdeburg* settled in the fog-shrouded sea the German destroyer V26 came crowding through the waves to perform a gallant rescue operation. The destroyer's captain ordered the boats to be lowered and the German sailors pulled away to pick up any of the *Magdeburg's* company still alive in the foam-crested waves. Before the destroyer's boats, overcrowded with men taken from the sea, could return shells were dropping among them. Gun flashes burst with smoky fire tints in the fog. Exploding shells echoed dully in the fog-laden air. Two Russian light cruisers, the *Bogatyr* and the *Pallada,* which had been shadowing the mine-layer, had swept up for the kill when it was realized what had happened to the *Magdeburg.* Their randomly planted shells blew several boats from the V26 clear out of the water. In turn the Russians began picking up survivors.

One sailor who was taken from the waves almost dead was clutching to his chest a curious book with weights inserted into its substantial binding. Had not the dying seaman held on to it while dying it would have sunk to the bottom of the Baltic. The dying German sailor's attempt to save the book was in time to save Ewing and his staff a great deal of challenging work.

When the Russian naval officers opened the book they found tables of figures and letters, arranged in apparently meaningless order until one of them grasped the incredible truth.

'It's the *Magdeburg's* code book,' he said.
They all continued staring at it until another said, 'What the devil are we going to do with it?'
'Send it to the High Command.'
'And will they know what to do with it?'

That was a joke deserving of a round of laughter, which it was duly accorded, and apparently justified, for the Russian Naval High Command not only did not know what to do with the German naval code book, but it wished to be rid of the responsibility for possessing it. 'The best thing we can do is send it to the British,' decided an admiral with broad rings of gold lace on his sleeve. 'They'll know what to do with it if anyone does.' This showed commendable trust in an ally's capacities, if lamentably little in one's own. However, the decision was taken and the *Magdeburg's* code book was dispatched by a very roundabout way to arrive in 40 OB, where Ewing, after the first probing glances at the pages of columns, suddenly became excited. He had reason to be.

By the time he and his team had broken the code they could decipher the mounds of monitored radio messages that had been pouring from Nauen's transmitting masts. They did not know it at the time but the work they were about to do was to result in the great naval Battle of Jutland.

They were still working on the *Magdeburg's* code book when the Germans brought a second high-powered radio station into operation. Allied direction finders soon located its position as the captured Belgian capital. This Brussels station began to compete with Nauen for the number of hours it was on the air. But when messages from it arrived in 40 OB the key provided by the *Magdeburg's* code book did not elucidate what appeared to be rows of gibberish. Ewing had a conference with his assistants and Admiral Hall. It was decided to ask the help of an Allied spy known to be working in Brussels. This agent was tagged as H523. Contact was made and a coded message delivered.

Agent H523 was entitled to consider he had been requested to perform the impossible. British Naval Intelligence wanted the code being used by the Germans in their radio transmissions from their station in Brussels.

Fortunately for Ewing and his colleagues awaiting results in 40 OB, agent H523 was not only a dedicated secret agent, but a well-trained professional. Before long it was known that a young Austrian technician was employed at the radio station. The Austrian doubled with his maintenance work the duties of a cipher clerk. His company was courted by H523, who did not take long in learning that the Austrian had a relative who had been born in England and was still living there. This relative held both British and Austrian citizenships.

At this stage some pressure was applied. The relative in England was located and she was persuaded by a British agent with a persuasive manner to write a letter to the relative in Brussels. She was told the letter would be delivered by hand, as indeed it was. In it she urged her relative to help the English who had been so kind and helpful to her. But any help given should be made in secret. The letter was so persuasive it might have been dictated by that British agent who called unexpectedly on her.

In time this letter was smuggled into Belgium by another agent operating in Holland, and the Austrian working at the radio station was given it by H523. There followed a large number of secret meetings in cafés and bars in the Belgian capital. The technician working as a cipher clerk became hard to convince that he should do as his relative in England requested. His reaction to being told that the best way to help the English was to copy out the station's radio code was near-panic: 'You know what would happen to me if I was found doing that?'

H523 knew very well. It was an open risk to which all spies were exposed by the very nature of their work. But a German firing squad did not seem to be the best topic to instil assurance in someone afraid of failing. 'You don't have to be found out,' the Austrian was reminded. 'Not if you are careful. Not, for instance, if you copied only one page at a time, or even part of a page, so that the pieces could be connected elsewhere. Think about it.'

H523 did a very good job of persuading the reluctant Austrian and a very brave one in remaining in close contact with the young man he had talked into becoming a spy for England. The radio station's code was copied slowly and tediously and delivered piece by piece to H523 at such times as the two could meet without attracting attention.

When the last lines of the secret German code had been passed over the Austrian was more scared than at any time previously, for now he realized that if the Germans for any reason suspected that their code had been broken they would know where to start looking and asking questions. He said nothing of his intentions to H523. He left his employment and vanished from Brussels. He had neither the heart nor the stomach to continue functioning as a spy. To be fair, he probably felt no reason to be dedicated to the life and its dangers. Anyway, he made a thoroughly good job of losing himself. Neither the Germans nor the British made contact with him again.

While he was covering his tracks Ewing and his men were working on those scraps of copied code that had been passed to H523. They were able to fill in some gaps in what they had already decoded. The final result was startling. Ewing found that one particular message referred to the All Highest, as the Germans spoke of their Kaiser. Apparently the All Highest had a pet plan and was pushing it. This was no less than to use the Imperial German Navy, hitherto bottled up in the Kiel Canal, to steam to the invasion of the East Anglian coast. Field Marshal von Hindenburg and Admiral von Tirpitz had both assured the Kaiser that, in their opinion, Britain's East Coast was virtually undefended from attack by sea.

When this message and its staggering implication was supplied to the Admiralty by 40 OB a swift and drastic change in the deployment of British capital ships was made in secret. In fact, a whole new naval defence policy was prepared. For this reason Jellicoe with the Home Fleet and Beatty with his battle-cruisers were able to steam fast to bring the German Grand Fleet to battle and engage them. Jutland might have been an indecisive battle in some respects, but the East Coast of England was saved from invasion, and the German fleet, mauled and crippled, scurried back to Kiel and safety. It did not venture to trade shots with the British enemy again during the war.

'Room 40, in decoding a German message,' said a commentator thirty-two years after Jutland, 'probably saved Britain and altered the world's history.' That rather drab room in the Admiralty's Old Building continued to function under Reginald Hall's direction as one of the sharpest weapons in the British tactical armoury. He himself made some crucial decisions.

One such decision was made in the year when Jutland was fought by advising the officers of the Crown in the trial of Sir Roger Casement[1] to publicize the notorious diaries kept by the man being tried for treason. In fact, as Chief of British Naval Intelligence, Reginald Hall had worked closely with Sir Basil Thomson and Scotland Yard's Special Branch in closing the trap that was sprung after Casement's return from Germany in a U-boat. Hall actually had the pages of the Casement diaries photographed. They were reproductions of these photographs that were dispatched to vociferous Irish nationalists in both the United States and Ireland, to the American Ambassador and the British Prime Minister and members of the Cabinet, as well as Members of Parliament, Church dignitaries, and others who would be influenced by their contents.

The genius of 40 O B had no deep feelings about whether Casement was tried as a traitor, for at this trade the man was ineffective and even pitiful, or as a second Oscar Wilde, whose perverted sexual instincts had made him a pariah in his own time, but Admiral Hall did object to a renegade

[1]See 'A Matter of High Treason' in the author's *Stories of Famous Modern Trials* (*Arthur Barker Ltd.*)

85

being hailed by politically minded partisans as a martyr at a time when Britain had her back to the wall and was fighting for survival and even democracy.

Another decision he took suggested that he had the awareness of a trained detective. That was after Wilhelm Wassmuss's personal baggage had reached London from as far away as the Middle East.,

Wilhelm Wassmuss was the German counterpart to Britain's Lawrence of Arabia. He was in the seaport of Bushire, on the Persian Gulf, when war came in 1914. Another of the Kaiser's dreams, besides the invasion of England's East Coast, which he had shelled in the war's early days, was the building of a Berlin-to-Bagdad railway, which would turn the eyes of Persia to a future shared with Germany, the dominant military power in Europe. Wilhelm Wassmuss had orders, as German vice-consul in Bushire, to further the cause of Germany among Persians and at the same time to discover all he could about the finances of those Persians who owned the country's oilfields. So active was Wassmuss as a German agent that the British tried time after time to capture him, and on one occasion an Arab chief who favoured the cause of the romantic Lawrence actually did trap the wily German. This was at Bebehen. The chief had been promised gold, and he must have been more concerned with the bright motes in his eye than the more realistic mirage of an angry German looking for a way to escape capture. For this reason the trap was sprung at the wrong moment, with a racing party of British unable to lay the German by his elusive heels after he had got clear of the Arabs.

Wassmuss only just made it, however, and he fled from the desert sands leaving his personal effects behind. He left something else before he was really clear from capture. This was a story that he had been furious at the loss of his baggage, most of which consisted of printed sheets of propaganda for Moslem consumption. Most Britishers who heard of Wassmuss's anger at losing his baggage found it cause for amusement. But not Reginald Hall of 40 OB. He decided it was cause for suspicion, asking himself why should any man be so demonstrably angry at losing printed propaganda sheets. He told Ewing, 'I want to locate Wass-muss's baggage. Will you have it found?'

The search did not take long. The stuff had been dumped not far away in London, still secured and strapped as it had been when left in the desert. It was brought to 40 OB and Hall and Ewing untied the straps. Concealed in items of apparel were two books, neither of which looked impressive. But one was a secret agent's book of ciphers and the other his detailed codes to which the ciphers were a series of skeleton keys. Once more 40 OB had its sphere of effective operation enlarged.

The sinking of the German mine-laying U-boat UC-44 was yet another piece of happy chance for the men in 40 OB. The submarine submerged, fatally wounded, in shallow coastal waters, and it was not long before the Royal Navy had a diver going down to examine the sunken craft. The diver had been trained to make such a search, and he knew what to look for. Moreover, he was not put off by a company of wide-eyed floating corpses in German naval uniforms. He found the submarine's book of codes and signals, in the familiar binding with weights. When he surfaced and handed over the secret volume to the expectant officer in the waiting launch he was told, 'Nice work'.

The work performed with that book by Ewing and his assistants was even nicer, from a purely Allied viewpoint. With the aid of the code and cipher books that had become the exclusive property of 40 OB, British Naval Intelligence were able to break down secret messages loaded with infor-mation proving that the denials of the German Ambassador in Washington, to the effect that his country was innocent of responsibility for acts of sabotage in the United States, were untrue. Moreover, Graf von Bernstorff was sending some of his coded messages back to Berlin along the American cables put at his disposal by the completely deceived American President, Woodrow Wilson.

This time Hall took a negative decision. He reasoned that what the Americans did not know could not harm the British at that moment in time. On the other hand, to inform them of what 40 OB had discovered at great pains would firstly leave the informant open to the charge of conspiring with a typically British trick to impair American relations with Germany, and secondly it would alert the Germans to the truth of how their codes and ciphers were no longer the secret to their enemies that they believed them to be.

Events shaped themselves to make a different decision truly timely. The *Lusitania* was torpedoed off Kinsale on the Southern Irish coast, with the loss of many lives, including American. There was a swift demand in the United States for its President, a man dedicated to peace at all costs, to undertake some rethinking now that American lives had been sacrificed to Germany's policy of indiscriminate submarine warfare. Reaction in the United States to the Cunarder's sinking was still news when Ewing came to his chief and showed him the latest disclosure forced from secret German messages by the researchers in 40 OB. This was no less than a long top-secret piece of information sent by Arthur Zimmermann, the German Foreign Minister in the Wilhelmstrasse, to von Eckhardt, the German Ambassador in Mexico. The message was concealed in another, considerably longer, and addressed to von Bernstorff, who was ordered to ensure that the shorter message was sent without delay and by a safe route to von Eckhardt. Von Bernstorff did as instructed. He sent the message for Mexico to the German Minister there. It was still in code when Western Union had it tapped over its wires on January 19th, 1917. The message to von Bernstorff was so important it had been sent in triplicate – by the American State Department's cable to be delivered on the President's instructions to the German Ambassador and by two radio routes, one from Nauen to the American commercial radio station at Sayville in New York State. Hall kept the secret cables and remained quiet.

At the end of January the Germans announced that indiscriminate submarine warfare was being resumed. It was as though the Wilhelmstrasse wanted to see how many snubs the American President would take. Well, he took this one for he too made an announcement: the United States was severing diplomatic relations with Germany. Anything, it seemed, short of open war.

Hall decided that the time had now come for the peace-loving Woodrow Wilson to realize that peace can be bought at too high a price. He had a conference with the British Foreign Secretary. As a result Hall approached Edward Bell, the Intelligence liaison officer attached to the staff of the American Ambassador in London. Bell appeared suspicious of what he read. So a direct approach was made to Ambassador Page, who decided to send the message to Washington, with the comment that if the message allegedly discovered by British Naval Intelligence was authentic, then it could be checked by the Zimmermann message to von Eckhardt that would be among the filed messages held by Western Union. To this end 40 OB would allow the Americans use of its secret code and cipher books for the deciphering of the message sent from Washington to London. The Americans would undertake the deciphering of the message in their own London Embassy.

It was a challenge that could not be left unaccepted, for this procedure would prove Hall was either a trickster or a man with a great many vital secrets to share. The challenge was accepted and in the American Embassy in London American decoders produced this from the Zimmermann message:

'We intend to begin unrestricted submarine warfare the 1st of February. We shall endeavour in spite of this to keep the United States neutral. In the event of this not succeeding, we make Mexico a proposal of alliance on the following bases: make war together, make peace together, general financial support, and an understanding on our part that Mexico is to reconquer the lost territory in Texas, New Mexico, and Arizona. The settlement in detail is left to you.

You will inform the President of the above most secretly as soon as the outbreak of the war with the United States is certain and the suggestion that he should on his own initiative invite Japan to immediate adherence and at the same time mediate between Japan and ourselves.

Please call the President's attention to the fact that the

unrestricted employment of our submarines now offers the prospect of compelling England to make peace within a few months.

Acknowledge receipt.

Zimmermann'.

Historically it was the most lethal attempt to stab the United States in the back prior to the Japanese attack without warning on Pearl Harbour. The scales were painfully torn from Woodrow Wilson's eyes when the truth was unveiled for him by his own decoders, one of whom was the sceptical Edward Bell. Within weeks the United States was at war.

8 The Lacemaker and the Frog

Among a crowd of civilian refugees that arrived in the Channel port of Folkestone in August 1914 was a young woman with red hair and smooth good looks. It was not surprising that she attracted the notice of an immigration officer who was scanning the newcomers, most of whom had fled before the advancing Germans. She had a personality that seemed to shine from her and not even the lack of normal feminine toilet facilities aboard the ship that had arrived overladen with fleeing humanity could dull that shine.

The task of the immigration officers was to question the refugees in the hope that a few of them carried information about the enemy that would be useful to the Allies. The immigration officer who caught the eye of the redhead beckoned to her and she squirmed her way through the throng to reach him.

'Monsieur?' she said.

He noticed that there was no plain band on the third finger of her left hand and smiled encouragingly.

'Mademoiselle,' he said in French, 'I should like to ask you a few questions. The answers might help us, you understand.'

'Certainly,' she said in English.

The man looking approvingly at her red hair and good looks showed surprise.

'You speak English, mademoiselle?'

'Yes,' she said. 'Also German.'

Then the questioning began. The officer learned that she had come from Lille, in the industrial north-east of France, which had been overrun by the grey-clad troops with coal-scuttle helmets. The woman, whose name was Louise de Bettignies, had been making for Saint-Omer to join her mother when she had been caught up in the retreating tide of refugees making for the coast. She was the daughter of a family of good standing that had come upon lean times. Her good education had enabled her to take the post of governess to several French families as well as several in Germany. There had been an occasion when she had been offered a post with the family of the Habsburg heir. She had declined it because Vienna was too far from her mother. However, in the space of fifteen years she had seen a very different life from the one she could afford. She had more often than not been treated by her employers as a member of their family. She had travelled with them, joined them at play, and even shared some of the family secrets. That shining look about Louise de Bettignies had been acquired in a way that made it a permanent acquisition. She had style and class and something that went even deeper than these: the stamp of quality as a human being.

The facts gleaned from the redheaded refugee were later considered by British Intelligence, who readily saw in her a possible agent if her story could be checked. The check on her could not be a full probe, but it was sufficiently thorough to provide a reasonable verification. She was again interviewed. This time by someone who came to her with a proposition: she was asked to return to Lille.

Her reaction was to wait calmly for the remainder of the request. She learned that she would be required to found an espionage cell with persons she knew and could vouch for, and if possible to get information through to the English commander, Sir John French, whose headquarters at that time was in Saint-Omer.

'It is vital that any change in the numbers and disposition of the German forces at this time is known by the British commander,' she was told. 'Possibly a woman would be better able to gather together such information than a man.'

She nodded, saying, 'I agree. But I have been told the Germans are very alert and suspicious of anyone observing their troops.'

'That is why it will take an exceptional person to succeed, Mademoiselle de Bettignies.'

She stared back calmly at the man who was laying it on the line for her. This time he waited, understanding that she was weighing her own courage in a personal balance. She said at last, with a little quaver in her voice, 'Very well, monsieur, I will return to France and do as you wish. I can only hope that I will not prove to be a disappointment.' The British Intelligence officer and the good-looking young woman who had just been recruited shook hands.

Within hours she was back in France and being taken to Saint-Omer, where she was welcomed by a mother who had grown fearful with waiting. Madame de Bettignies's pleasure was short-lived, for Louise did not delay in explaining that she had to return to Lille. 'My God – why, Louise?' her mother demanded. 'It is madness. The town is in the hands of the Germans. You'd have to pass through their lines.' Madame de Bettignies was told part of the reason that had brought her daughter back to France. She seemed paralysed by the news, unable to rise from her chair or to speak. She sat looking at Louise as though she saw a ghost and kept saying over and over in a whisper, 'Oh, no. Oh, no. Oh, no.'

Unhappily because the news had brought such grief to her mother, Louise sought the aid of a priest who had been her confessor. This was a *curé* named Boulange, to whom she revealed more fully how she had committed herself and what her actions could mean and the demands that might be made of her. It was a moment in her life when Louise de Bettignies needed spiritual support. Presumably the *curé* was able to give her that support as well as his blessing, because a short while later she was at the headquarters of the GOC, British Expeditionary Force. There she was told what was expected of her and thanked for her readiness to work as a spy. Arrangements were made for the reception of information she would send. After that she started the long route back to Lille.

She was taken to Folkestone again, kitted out with various supplies and money to defray necessary expenses, and then under cover of darkness she crossed to Holland and arrived in Vlissingen, otherwise Flushing, on the south edge of the island of Walcheren, from where she crossed to Breskens on the mainland. A few kilometres to the south-west was the Belgian frontier, fenced off and guarded by troops equipped with searchlights to pierce the darkness of the small hours when a desperate person might try to cross the shiny wire that was beginning to darken with rust. If such a desperate person dallied on the Belgian side of the wire he could step on a trip wire that would explode a buried mine.

Not far from this wire, still on the Dutch side, Louise, wearing dark clothes, was met by a Belgian named Verstapen, who had been alerted by the British. He was known to be a smuggler in the former days and nights of peace and was as conversant with the Dutch-Belgian border as a rabbit. Indeed, although he was a big man, he resembled a rabbit in the way he led Louise to a concealed trench that actually ran under the Germans' wire. Louise de Bettignies, feeling rather like Alice in Wonderland, had felt her hand taken after passwords had been exchanged, and then had been helped down into the trench that had been covered with turfs and leaves at its concealed entrance. In a damp and crowding darkness, feeling cold and scared, she followed this big man with cold hands who smelled pungently of earth and stained clothing. He led her to another concealed entrance to that winding underground tunnel, helped her out, and after covering the entrance again led the trembling woman away from the nightmare of the fence and the concealed minefield.

Slowly she took confidence from the assurance of Alphonse Verstapen, who had lived with varying degrees of danger since a child. He led her along narrow country roads barely visible in a thin starlight until it was daylight, when they concealed themselves and made a cold meal. Afterwards they set off across Belgium in a south-westerly direction, making for Lille. Both the man and the woman had forged identity documents provided by the British. These had to be shown to sentries on the outskirts of towns through which they passed. They crossed the frontier with France between Ypres and Mons and eventually arrived in Lille, but it scarcely felt to Louise like coming home. Much of the town had been destroyed by German gunfire. Familiar landmarks were heaps of rubble. Louise made her way to the south-west part of the town and in the Rue d'Isly stopped at a door and rang the bell. The summons was answered by a woman who looked what she was, a servant. For a moment she stared frowningly at the two visitors, and then clapped her hands: 'Mademoiselle de Bettignies!'

Verstapen stayed for a meal and then left when the street was pronounced clear by the servant Louise addressed as Clothilde. Louise slept that night in a room that was familiar because it had been hers not very long before, although it seemed now to belong to another life.

The next morning she took from a cupboard a handbag she had once discarded. Into this she dropped the identity card and papers that described her as Alice Dubois. She went out and bought needles and crochet hooks and cotton thread, which were dropped into the old brown handbag. She walked slowly through the town, watching the troops marching to the front. She talked to people in the street markets, phrasing her questions with care and picking up pieces of information that could be useful to the forces opposed to the Germans. Before she arrived back in the Rue d'Isly she had been stopped by a German patrol and asked for her papers. From the brown handbag she took the folded card of stiff unglazed paper. 'Alice Dubois,' read out the German sergeant, 'lacemaker.' He tapped the bag. 'Let me see inside.' He stared at the needles and thread and some bread Louise had bought, thrust the identity card at her, and waved her on. That night Louise sat up late clicking the needles, creating a length of lace as fine as any knitted by the women who sit making lace by the canals criss-crossing Bruges, grateful to her mother for teaching her the art.

Louise's task was to gather information about enemy

troops not only in the township of Lille, but in the entire industrial complex of which Lille is the centre. This meant travelling to such other towns as Roubaix, Tourcoing, and Tournai, being challenged by German guards and sentries, showing her lace and identity card, and explaining that she had to travel to be able to sell the lace she made. As Valenciennes, noted for its lace, was a town not far away her claim evoked no suspicion. She was able to learn a good deal about the troops the Germans had moved into the Arras sector of the Western Front.

Very gradually she made contacts who agreed to help her in her work as a spy. Marie Léonie Vanhoutte was one of the first and she became Louise's chief assistant. The two women met in a shop. Marie-Léonie became Charlotte in the band of helpers Louise collected. As Charlotte she too went around the countryside, lugging a basket with cheeses under a square of white linen. She had a peasant's broad open face, which helped her as a seller of local cheeses.

But Louise also required assistants whose addresses could be places for the use of special equipment. Part of this urgent need was supplied when in the West Flanders town of Mouscron, which had a textile industry, she met a chemist named de Geyter. Not only the chemist, but his wife also, proved very ready to be enlisted in Louise's secret work as spy. They offered their home as a meeting-place, and the husband set up a secret laboratory for making invisible inks, for printing propaganda sheets,[1] for photographic work and radio repairs. Transport was provided by the Sions, father and son, until the Germans requisitioned the vehicles.

Information began to flow across No Man's Land to the British lines. At last the troops facing the Germans were no longer men fighting an imagined foe. The British General Staff received from the secret agent news about what was happening behind the German strands of barbed wire, which regiments were living like moles in the Flanders mud, which artillery batteries were being brought up to increase the barrage being laid down.

[1]See also 'The White Lady and Others' in the author's *Stories of Famous Spies* (Arthur Barker Limited).

The war was suddenly and continuously a very real commitment for the redhead who had been a governess and was now officially a lacemaker. She began to include in her spy circle some very useful agents. Such as a former police chief named Lenfant in Tourcoing, who was able to advise her on certain aspects of security. Persons of means, like Madame Prouvost-Maturel, who lived on a secluded estate, and persons who worked hard for three meals a day and a bottle of *vin ordinaire*, like Alphonse Verstapen, joined her underground espionage movement that grew daily. But with growth came more dangerous odds. The chance of discovery became greater as the number of Alice Dubois's helpers increased.

Although she approved of no new volunteers until she had explained the risks involved and the need for secrecy if disaster struck, she became haunted by a fear that loomed as a certainty. On the simple law of averages discovery of one link in her finely constructed chain must occur eventually, for she knew very well that the Germans had their own competent counter-espionage system working throughout the full area of the Lille complex of industrial towns. But until that day the group controlled by Louise continued to function with widening scope. After major battles night trains with lowered blinds bearing German wounded back to the fatherland were counted and a reasonable estimate made of casualties that had been inflicted and of replacements that would be necessary. It was not sufficient merely to know these figures. They had to be supported by basic arithmetic, and the result delivered in British hands, because a correct evaluation meant vital changes being made in the British lines.

On one such occasion, following upon a battle that had lasted for many days, Louise decided the only way of getting the statistics into British hands was for her to take them, prepared in detail. But she could not possibly go through the German lines. She would have to recross Belgium and reach England by way of Holland. To do this would not only be dangerous, especially getting into the neutral Netherlands, but she would be open to discovery by a German agent or a

Dutch national who might be friendly to the Germans. De Geyter, the chemist, prepared a fresh identity card for her and also a passport to be used in Holland. A professional map-maker named Paul Bernard undertook the task of transcribing the equivalent of three thousand words on to a piece of transparent paper no larger than a lens in a pair of spectacles. This was done, first, by reducing the wordage by adopting a shorthand system. This was conveyed to the paper, in invisible ink supplied by de Geyter, by working with a very finely nibbed calligraphic pen and observing the results through a strong magnifying lens, also supplied by the Mouscron chemist. Louise had to make allowances not only for being stopped and questioned, but even searched. She could not imagine a better hiding-place than the transparent paper over a spectacle lens. It was a device worthy of Edgar Allan Poe, but whereas Poe's inventions were for mere fictional presentation, Louise's were to stand the hard scrutiny of dangerous reality, with the price for failure a bullet from a German Mauser rifle.

On this occasion she was again conducted across the Dutch frontier without being discovered, and she crossed from Flushing to Folkestone, two towns with regular sailing schedules to each other, closely watched by German agents, without arousing the suspicion of a secret onlooker. Major Cameron, the officer who met her at a secret rendezvous in the Kentish seaport, had a task peeling the transparent paper from a lens of her spectacles without impairing it or the message crowded with important data, but within hours she was back in Lille and the British were making necessary alterations to their front-line dispositions.

Yet another detailed list of logistic statistics was copied on to a similar piece of transparent paper by Bernard, working with de Geyter's equipment. The paper was cut into an oblong that fitted over Louise's photo on a fresh identity card. The paper gave the photo additional gloss, which made acquiring a German 'pass' stamp that much simpler, but the ink on the German stamp almost ruined the message on the transparent paper. It took the British many patient hours to secure that message later, and before those hours had run their course Louise was back in the Rue d'Isly, her old brown handbag again in the cupboard where she had found it.

Then came her first meeting with the Frog, the squat-figured German woman who had been a police matron. It occurred on a dark night, when she was walking to the house of one of her helpers with another invisible message that had been transcribed on to a cigarette paper. She carried a simple peasant's lantern of the kind that is really a covered candlestick with glass panels. It was the guttering candleflame that alerted a German patrol who sprang out at her. She screamed and protested, but was taken to a building where she came face to face with the Frog.

'Well?' demanded the German woman who might or might not have known that the French had dubbed her *la Grenouille*.

'Just a moment,' said the seemingly scared Louise. 'I can't afford to waste a candle.'

She opened the door of the cheap lantern and blew out the candle's flame.

'Strip,' said the Frog, not amused by this display of Gallic frugality, even in such unlikely circumstances.

Louise's clothes and body were thoroughly searched, with a negative result. Grudgingly she was told she could go. She dressed and then asked for a light for her candle before she stepped into the dark. The Frog handed her a box of matches. Only when Louise reached her destination was the candle split down with a knife and the concealed piece of cigarette paper bearing the invisible message removed.

A legend about Louise's resourcefulness grew up in the ranks of the underground movement she controlled. She was admired because she refused to run unnecessary risks, and in this way schooled her helpers in the same care for how they operated. She did not duplicate a successful subterfuge unless it was vitally necessary. She strove to find new ways of deceiving the enemy. It is said that once when carrying a message to a distribution point she had it concealed in the middle of a ball of black wool. A German patrol called to her to stop. Before the patrol caught up with her she had tossed the ball of wool into a hedge and left one end hanging over the front of the place of concealment. After being closely questioned by the patrol and having her clothing searched she was left alone and the patrol moved off. As soon as it was safe she returned to the hedge, groped for the free end of her ball of black wool, and then found the part that concealed her message.

Louise came, in time, to be recognized as the possessor of one of the most agile brains working secretly for the Allies against the Germans. Countless stories were told of the risks she ran and the ingenuity displayed in eluding capture. The Germans once commandeered her shoes, left outside a hotel room to be cleaned. The Germans did not find the message hidden in a heel, but the next morning the shoes were brought to her brightly shone by the soldier who had removed them for 'inspection'. Such hazards were calculated to age a normal person but Louise de Bettignies seemed to thrive on living dangerously.

The next time she met the Frog was when she and Charlotte had been rounded up by a patrol and were searched by the German woman. Charlotte offered the sharp-eyed female guard a piece of chocolate. Louise held her brown handbag out to her, but clung to a piece of freshly bought sausage. The Frog skinned the sausage and mashed it, but found nothing. She threw away the chocolate into the handbag, which she gave to Louise. Away from that inspection house Louise removed a message from where it was concealed in a seam of the bag's base.

There were a number of similar occurrences before the luck of Louise de Bettignies ran out. Today they are parts of the fabric of a lasting legend. For more than three years she ran the gauntlet of German determination to stop a leak they suspected in the Lille area. When they were tired of being unsuccessful they sent Major Rotselaer to the district. He was accompanied by several officers experienced in counter-espionage.

Some time afterwards, when Louise was in the Netherlands, Marie-Léonie Vanhoutte, otherwise Charlotte received by the morning post a postcard from Louise which in code announced all was well, and a letter in an unknown handwriting. It told Charlotte that she was to lose no time in going to the Lion Belge on a matter that concerned 'Alice'.

She thought the letter could be a trap in view of what was said on the postcard, but the use of the code name 'Alice' made her fear that something had gone wrong and she must find out what. She walked to the *auberge* called the Lion Belge and was approached by a cleanshaven stranger who said he had important news from Alice. Charlotte denied knowing anyone of that name. Early next morning she was roused from sleep by banging on her front door. In the street were two men with revolvers drawn. One was the stranger from outside the Lion Belge.

She was taken away while the house was being searched and was put in a cell at the prison of St Gilles in Roubaix. She was still in that cell when Louise returned from Holland, was told of the arrest, and at once made arrangements for how her group should continue to function in the event of her own arrest, which now seemed likely. Afterwards she prepared her latest report, which was committed to a piece of cigarette paper by Bernard. This she concealed between a ring she invariably wore and the flesh of her finger. Word was sent to a female contact to meet her at a point between Tournai and Mouscron, and the woman was to provide herself with a travel permit. The woman was over-confident and arrived without the permit. Louise was extremely angry at this flagrant omission to obey an explicit instruction. After reducing the other to tears she herself went past a sentry by showing her own permit and holding a thumb over her name. The woman without a permit was left standing near a house not far from the sentry's post. Stopping at a house on the other side of the raised barrier, Louise gave her permit to a small boy and told him to take it past the sentry to the woman waiting by the house. The boy hid the permit in his shoe, reached the woman, and gave her Louise's permit, with which she passed the sentry. But the two women had not gone far when they were stopped by two men in plain clothes, who asked for their papers. Louise's permit was in the other woman's bag, so she pretended she had mislaid her own. At that moment the de Geyters were seen coming down the street, and to create a diversion Louise hailed them. Acting on Louise's own instructions that had been repeated many times, the husband and wife said they did not know her. All four were put into a car with curtained windows and taken to the St Gilles prison. Isolated in a cell of her own, Louise recovered the message from under her ring and began to chew it. Then she found she was being watched.

'Give me what you have in your mouth,' ordered the man who appeared.

'I haven't anything in my mouth. I just feel scared,' she said.

The man went away and returned accompanied by the Frog, who took a quick glance at Louise and told the man she knew this woman. Several times she had examined her without finding anything suspicious. Suddenly the Frog was smiling, which seemed out of character. She told Louise she would fetch her a warm drink to help calm her, but Louise refused the steaming glass of milk that was produced. When the man became furious she knew it would have been fixed with an emetic to make her sick and disgorge the chewed message. He insisted that she drink the glass of milk.

'Very well,' said Louise, taking the glass with a hand that appeared to be trembling violently. The glass slipped from her shaking fingers before it reached her mouth. At that the Frog lost her sudden and strange air of benevolence. She grabbed the prisoner's arm and took her to another cell on the door of which was written in white chalk in German: 'A dangerous prisoner'. An hour later the Frog came back with Charlotte. Both said they did not know the other. The Frog and Major Rotselaer thought otherwise.

Days passed while the German counter-espionage service worked the clock round to secure scraps of evidence about both women. When they were brought to trial charged with actively spying mere denials were useless. Both were found guilty as charged and sentenced to death. Louise requested the court in German to spare the life of her companion, and added that she herself was quite prepared to die. Charlotte did not understand German, but she heard her name spoken and guessed from Louise's manner what was being said. She hurriedly asked the court in French to spare Louise's life.

On what was to be their last morning word came that the German Governor, von Bissing, who had earned world-wide hatred for not commuting Edith Cavell's sentence of death, had changed his mind. Louise's sentence was changed to life imprisonment, and Charlotte's to fifteen years'. Within a few hours both were on their way to Germany. Louise de Bettignies was sent to a prison in Cologne, where some time later she caught typhus. The disease killed her. She died on 27 September 1918, about seven weeks before the British Brigade of Guards marched into the city. Her liberators, whose cause she had served well and faithfully, were too late to save her. But they found her grave and her body was taken from enemy soil to a last resting-place in France, where it was reinterred with full military honours after being accompanied by a cushion bearing the four medals she had been awarded posthumously, two by England and two by France.

Marie-Léonie Vanhoutte survived to return to her shop in Roubaix and retell the full story of 'Alice Dubois, lacemaker'.

9 On the Wrong Wavelength

Although the Germans succeeded in learning little from Louise de Bettignies herself they saw her story as a lesson to be learned, and when war came again, twenty-five years after the gallant Frenchwoman stepped ashore at Folkestone to face British immigration officers, the lesson had been thoroughly taken to heart. It was this: sending a spy as a refugee stood a great chance of succeeding. Moreover, if the bogus refugee went with a good cover story that could not easily be broken, then there was every chance that he would be taken at his own evaluation.

The Nazis tried this technique a number of times. To their surprise they had a surprising number of failures, which were dangerous for the men who had prepared for success. Two of those failures include a pair of radio spies who became notorious. One was a Belgian, the other a Dutchman. In fairness to the former, he was a spy against his patriotic inclinations and was coerced into working for the Germans who for the second time had overrun his country. The latter was a very different man. He proved himself a ready tool for promise of generous payment by masters who he was sure would emerge victors later.

Joseph Jan Vanhoven was twenty-seven and a waiter in a Brussels hotel, where he had to serve the German officers whose arrogance made him writhe internally. It was a German lieutenant who bothered to treat him with a modicum of courtesy and as a human being with private feelings. Lieutenant Eilenburg, as a matter of fact, seemed to realize that the man who served him with plentiful plates of food was in truth close to starving. The Germans had grabbed most of the country's food supplies and the ordinary Belgian lived on severely restricted rations, a good deal of them of the notorious *ersatz* quality.

One day after being served the lieutenant put down the newspaper he had been reading and said, 'I've news for you, Vanhoven.' The waiter stood very still, wondering what he had done to earn being singled out in this way, for he very naturally feared the worst. Instead, the lieutenant told him he should present himself to the quartermaster of the German troops in that area and ask for a certain person by name. 'Tell him you've come from Lieutenant Eilenburg,' the German explained. 'He'll know what to do. You'll come away with food and something to smoke.'

It sounded too good to be true. Vanhoven had elderly parents who were particularly hard hit by the German rationing system. The next day he followed the lieutenant's advice, went to the quartermaster's stores and asked for the man whose name he had been given. To his surprise he found he was expected. The man went away and returned with a bulky parcel of food and a generous supply of cigarettes. 'Here you are,' he said. 'This has been put aside for you. Take it.' Vanhoven caught the wrapped-up packages to his chest and started to thank the man who had passed them to him. The man did not stop to receive the other's thanks. The Belgian left the camp. No one stopped him. No one challenged him. He did not know it, but he had been caught like a fly in a spider's web.

The next day when the lieutenant appeared at his customary table Vanhoven started to thank him profusely, but was waved to silence. 'You can have such supplies regularly,' Lieutenant Eilenburg told him, looking over his bowl of soup, 'if you're prepared to do something with them.' He took several spoonfuls from the bowl before adding in a low voice, 'I mean dispose of them on the black market. You understand?'

Vanhoven understood very well. He knew he had been trapped. If he refused the lieutenant would be an enemy who would find a way of removing him, a very simple matter for a German officer in an occupied country. On the other hand, if he agreed, he might be walking into further trouble, but at least he would be able to count on the patronage of the lieutenant, who would be involved.

'I understand,' he said.

'Good, then that is settled.'

The lieutenant went on to enjoy his meal. At the end, when he took the bill from the waiter, he said, 'We share fifty-fifty the money you obtain. I consider that generous of me.'

So the waiter began the collection of packaged foodstuffs from the German quartermaster's staff, which he sold on the thriving Belgian black market. It has been claimed that the lieutenant made a considerable sum from such trading, and that Vanhoven handed him, at one time and another, more than fifty thousand Belgian francs. But the lieutenant was not satisfied by being on to a good thing. Like many crooks he wanted to use his gains. He took a train to Paris one time when he had leave and arrived back in Brussels with a fur coat, which had been noted by the Germans at the customs post. Word was sent to the German counter-espionage service, who were curious about where the lieutenant was finding a means of augmenting his pay. They came to a false conclusion and summoned Lieutenant Eilenburg to a meeting at which he was asked directly if he was supplying information to enemy agents. The lieutenant's composure was brutally fractured. He blurted out the truth, claiming that he had started the racket because he was infatuated with a dancer in Germany who would only show him favour if he continued to provide her with costly gifts.

Suddenly Lieutenant Eilenburg no longer sat at his table any more in the dining-room of the Cosmopolitan Hotel and there were no more food parcels for Vanhoven to pick up. Instead, the waiter was arrested at the hotel and taken to Gestapo headquarters. His interrogator was Hans Junglau, who told him that, for selling German Army food on the black market he could be shot. When he started to relate Lieutenant Eilenburg's role in the illicit trading he was interrupted by a brief announcement.

'We have dealt with the lieutenant. He has been transferred to where he will have no further opportunity to line
his pocket in this criminal fashion. Now you, Vanhoven.
You can be shot or you can co-operate and be helpful. The
choice is yours.'
'How can I be helpful?' the trembling waiter inquired.
'Simply by doing what we tell you. Listen closely.'

What Vanhoven heard in that room at Gestapo
headquarters raised goose pimples on his flesh. As in a daze
he heard himself say, 'I'll do it. I'll co-operate.'

The next day he did not appear at his customary time at
the hotel. The morning newspapers carried a story saying
that he had fled to avoid a charge of black marketeering. He
was actually being bumped in a Gestapo car that was racing
him to Paris, where he was released after receiving very
careful instructions. He found his way to the French underground movement with clippings from the Brussels papers
about his flight, which established that he was a genuine
fugitive. He was helped across France and into Spain, guided
by smugglers. Before long he arrived at the German Embassy
in Madrid, where he found the German Ambassador,
Eberhard von Stohrer, awaiting him. He was treated with
marked kindness and consideration, given money, and told
he should relax and take a short holiday. Meantime the
smiling German wanted all the Belgian could tell him about
the French underground that he had learned on the journey
to the Spanish frontier. Vanhoven had to sing for not only
his supper, but for each meal he ate while in Spain. He
enjoyed none of them.

At length he was summoned to receive orders that had
arrived from Germany. He was to be smuggled into Britain
as a refugee. Once in London his task would be explained in
detail, but he was informed that he was to operate a secret
radio.

A Spanish ship with a cargo of oranges took him to
Stockholm, where he was allowed to 'escape', in due course
to enter the front door of another embassy. This time it was
the British in Strandvägen. He was given an attentive

audience after presenting his Belgian identity card and telling his well-rehearsed story of escape to freedom. The newspaper clippings supported his story of taking German food to help his starving fellow-countrymen.

'What do you wish to do?' he was asked.
'Join the Belgians in Britain.'

Vanhoven remained in Sweden while coded messages sped between Sweden and Britain. The worst of his fears left him when he was accompanied to a plane that was within minutes airborne and heading westward. He had been told the British and Belgian authorities would welcome him. They did. However, the experienced men at Scotland Yard did not accept his story at face value. Two things about it seemed suspicious to them. One, it was all very smooth and uncomplicated. Almost too easy to accept. Two, this new refugee arrived with all his necessary paperwork to support his story. Most refugees had trouble getting out of Europe, and arrived with gaps in their stories that had to be filled in by careful checking. Vanhoven's story was seemingly water-tight, almost as though it had been prepared in advance.

These suspicions were not hinted at, however during the Belgian's interviews at the Yard. He was cleared, as he thought. He did not know that when he left the Yard he was followed.

A few days later he made his way to London's East End, where he entered a public-house whose name and address had been given to him by von Stohrer. After a couple of glasses of beer he asked if he could speak to Mr Pearson, but was told no one of that name was known. That seemed to be a dead end until someone asked him to have a drink and took him into a corner of the bar. 'I know Mr Pearson,' said the stranger.

When Vanhoven left the pub he had learned that he was to join a community of Belgian sailors in London and had been briefed how to go about this. What he did not know was that his arrival at the pub had labelled him as a spy to Scotland Yard, which had known for some time that the place was a vital link in a chain of German communication with their spies. It had not been raided because the Yard wanted the place to continue as normal, so that it could be kept under close surveillance.

Vanhoven began work as an active spy. He was accepted by the Belgian sailor community, shared what they knew of ships and their sailing dates and destinations, and eventually he was put to work with a transmitter. It was not provided by the mysterious Mr Pearson, whom he did not meet because he did not exist.

When Vanhoven, acting on his secret instructions, had collected some helpers who were ready to take German payment so long as it was substantial he was suddenly arrested and taken into custody. His nerve cracked beyond mending. This time it was not a black market offence with the threat of death as a possible punishment. He had been uncovered as a spy in wartime. Death was the price he had to pay.

He endeavoured to forestall the inevitable by making a full confession. He was heard out by stone-faced men who had learned through long years not to be impressed by confessions that are made after discovery. He was kept in prison until his trial and then he was heard again. The court passed a verdict of guilty and he was sentenced to death. He pleaded for his life, only to discover that to the stone-faced men he was already dead. He was not kept long living on borrowed time. He was hanged and his file closed. Vanhoven was one of eighteen German spies hanged in Britain during the war. The sentence delivered to him by Mr Justice Hallett at the Old Bailey on 24 May 1944 was carried out at Pentonville two months later.

Without being aware of the fact he had joined the company of the man who became known as the BBC spy, Johannes Marinus Dronkers. Dronkers was not a recruited amateur like the Belgian. He was a Dutch Nazi. He had been born near Utrecht on 3 April 1896, and had joined the Dutch Merchant Service after leaving school and been trained as a ship's telegraphist. He had also learned English and was reasonably fluent in the language, though he spoke with a guttural accent.

Not long after his fortieth birthday he decided he had seen enough of the world and its seaports and applied for a post with the Dutch Post Office. When Holland was invaded by the Germans in 1939 such a man was ready-made for employment by the conquerors who wore swastikas on their left arms. But although Dronkers proved himself a ready tool for the Nazis, he had little idea that he was to be employed on a mission that was the pet dream of one of Admiral Canaris's most forward-looking aides. This was General Joseph von Tippelskirch, who wanted to find a willing and co-operative agent to work with the British Broadcasting Corporation: a brilliant if insolent notion, to have a German spy broadcasting information from the BBC in London.

After discussion with Canaris himself, von Tippelskirch decided the only chance of achieving this very desirable aim was to pick a national of one of the invaded countries, smuggle the man into Britain, and have him approach his Government's office in London and offer himself as a broadcaster to his own countrymen in Europe. Such a man could broadcast anti-German propaganda which could conceal coded messages. But first it meant finding the right man, who had to be suitable in every way.

This task was given to the man who was accepted as Dr Ranken by Gestapo headquarters in Berlin. He was Nicolaus Adolf Ritter. He told von Tippelskirch, 'I believe the best man for this mission is a Dutchman who is a Nazi.' 'Very well,' he was told. 'Find him.'

Although Dronkers was in the Netherlands waiting to be found, as a known Nazi he was carefully avoiding exposure. The Dutch Resistance had sprung to growth with mushroom-like rapidity almost overnight, and although German Nazis stood on street corners the home-grown product was being cautious not to risk being dealt with in secret.

It was Teutonic thoroughness that finally uncovered the unknown man for whom von Tippelskirch sought. Nicolaus Ritter approached the Gestapo chief in the Netherlands. This was SS General Walter Rauter, whose local headquarters was in The Hague. He explained what he wanted. 'I'll ask the leaders of the Dutch National Socialist Party,' Rauter said, 'to recommend a good man.' He spoke to Adrian Mussert, the Dutch Nazi Führer, who took his time compiling a list of candidates for the job. Among the names was that of Johannes Marinus Dronkers. Dronkers' name was ticked as a special recommendation.

The man was found and taken to a meeting with his would-be employers. The scheme for getting him into Britain, with the intention of having him accepted as a broadcaster on the BBC's service to occupied Europe, was explained: 'Of course, you will volunteer. You will be well rewarded and there will be a bright future for you.'

Dronkers preferred snapping at the carrot to feeling the weight of the stick. He readily volunteered and was told his financial reward would be a very considerable sum – if he lived to receive it (the proviso was not mentioned). 'You will be sent for special training to one of our specialist schools,' he was told. That promise was speedily kept, and within hours Dronkers was being reshaped and made over into someone who was not himself. A stranger, in effect, who posed as Johannes Marinus Dronkers. For that was the policy decision taken by the men attempting to make von Tippelskirch's dream come true. Ritter, for one, was convinced that agents had been lost because, established in Britain, they had been careless in not adhering meticulously to a cover story that had been prepared, with faked personality, changed name and parentage and altered background. A slip had aroused suspicion, and the English worried suspicion, as a dog did a bone, until it surrendered the hidden meat and marrow.

This was not to happen in the case of Dronkers. He was to retain his own name, his family, his background, so that he had no two answers to such questions as 'Where was your father employed?' or 'What was your mother's birthday?' In that way he could not be caught off-guard, nor could he be guilty of a minor slip that could be checked against a previously recorded fact.

So it was that Dronkers was changed inside, rather than outside. He was made into a spy with special training. He was tested until he was asleep on his feet, but he always gave the correct answer, even with only part of his brain working for him. The only secret that had to remain buried in his consciousness was the purpose of his 'escaping' to Britain. He was drilled by ruthless drill-masters until he was flawless. He became to the pleased Ritter the perfect spy. The secret agent whose cover could not be broken because it was genuine.

He was finally accepted as ready to start on his mission in May 1942, cheered by the thought that he would earn a wage vastly in excess of any paid to a regular BBC news reader. On the 17th of the month he was carefully cast adrift in a small sailing yacht with a Dutch horizontal tricolor at the stern. The small craft took advantage of a light breeze and headed west across the North Sea, to be sighted in the early hours of the 18th by a British trawler, which changed course and drew close to the bobbing yacht.

A man in the yacht was waving a small flag and obviously trying to attract attention. He had a Dutch sou'wester covering his head and a Dutch fisherman's oilskins over his clothes. The trawler's skipper had a boat lowered and the obviously excited man in the yacht was brought aboard, where he threw up his arms and legs in a wild caper of delight and began to sing *Tipperary*.

The armed trawler's skipper waited until the song was finished before asking the newcomer's name. He was told he had picked up Johannes Marinus Dronkers, one-time second mate aboard a Dutch freighter, who had been employed in the Utrecht post office until the Gestapo had arrested him. He was asked how he had got away and said he had made his way to Helleveet-Sluis, where he had been given the yacht by a Dutch friend, and had escaped under cover of darkness.

When asked if he had any documents to prove his story he ripped open a seam of his sou'wester and removed the customary identity card and other papers as well as a letter purporting to be from the headquarters of the Dutch Resistance in Utrecht. The letter outlined the part he had taken in helping the Resistance, which had resulted in his arrest by the local Gestapo, from whom he had escaped with assistance from comrades in the Underground. Included in this revealing letter was a recommendation, to the British and Dutch Governments, because he was now a marked man wanted by the Germans.

Some hours later Dronkers was in a glass-enclosed office not far from the quay at Harwich, being questioned closely by Intelligence officers. They could not trick him into an obviously false or suspicious admission, and for their part he was given clearance.

But there were still counter-espionage men, some trained in the Yard's Special Branch, waiting to interview him, more subtle in approach, more devious in method, with a vast backlog of information from which they could check anything he said. He faced them in London, and without comment he was passed over to the Dutch Security Service, staffed by tough patriotic Hollanders only too ready to smell out a planted spy. It was at this interview that his letter from the Utrecht Resistance leader was checked and the signature at its foot compared with another. The signature was pronounced genuine, which fact provides its own comment upon the quality of the forgers employed by the Germans in their espionage schools.

When Dronkers was informed that he had been passed as genuine he began another dance of delight, and offered to work as a broadcaster for Radio Oranje, the official Dutch Government station broadcasting from a BBC transmitter. 'I know what will lift our people's morale,' he boasted. 'Believe me, I'll tell them the truth about the Germans in our streets. They'll know I've recently been among them.'

He was told it sounded like a good idea and wished good-day. In Intelligence all good ideas are well tested. Back down the line went the word that this newcomer Dronkers wanted to broadcast to his fellow-countrymen. Up came the comment, 'Let him.'

Accordingly, within a few days of his spirited request being made to the Dutch Security Service, Dronkers was told he had been accepted as a broadcaster. He was collected and taken to a building in London where he was kept waiting in a small room before a pretty female secretary opened the door and said, 'Johannes Marinus Dronkers? Will you please follow me?' She spoke in Dutch.

He followed her down a narrow corridor to an office equipped with a microphone. Several Dutchmen turned to greet him with smiles and congratulations. He was made to feel at his ease. There could be no question in his mind that everything was going as he wished. When he was waved to the chair before the microphone he was so happy he could have laughed. He had fooled his own people and the British and was on the point of demonstrating to his German masters over a wavelength that would be monitored at The Hague that they had chosen wisely when they selected Johannes Marinus Dronkers. He knew precisely how he would bury a secret message in his broadcast. After that it would merely be a matter of waiting for further instructions and obeying them. No one would ever know until after the war how he had helped towards a complete Nazi victory and the subjugation of the defiant English in their tight little isle.

Lights flickered on a panel. A clock with a large second hand was watched. He was given a signal, and suddenly there was no dryness in his mouth, no slight taut feeling in his throat. He was speaking fluently and smoothly and with every show of confidence. He kept his eye on the panel with lights and on the clock and the hand of the man who would signal when his time was coming to a close.

Then it was over and he knew with full certitude of mind and spirit that he had done a good job. He turned around in his chair to receive the congratulations of the other Dutchmen. He was startled to find their places taken by three men who were not Dutch and who certainly were not smiling. One of them said, 'We should like you to come with us.'

There was something ominous about the words and the way they were spoken. Dronkers had trouble getting up from the chair, but quickly pulled himself together. 'Certainly, gentlemen,' he said with forced cheerfulness. However, the cheerfulness didn't last. He was informed that his 'broadcast' had not gone out live. No one outside a room with Intelligence men seated to make notes had heard his words, which would be gone over time and again to find if they

114

concealed anything hidden in them. Then the fresh questions began.

Why had he been so insistent on a broadcaster's job? Why? Why had he gone out of his way to explain that he would make a good broadcaster? Why had he been so pleased to be told he would be given such a job? How did he come to have such a good broadcasting voice, almost as though he had been trained?

The questions went on ceaselessly, in Dutch by grim Dutchmen, in English by equally grim Englishmen. Soon the man being questioned was sweating, his mind became confused, and he tried to justify himself, and that was when he was caught in his first slip. Others followed. When they were pointed out he broke down, confessed the truth, and then explained the code designed specially for use in broadcasting in Dutch.

On 13 November he appeared at the Old Bailey before Mr Justice Wrottesley, was found guilty, and after an appeal had been dismissed a month later he was executed at Wandsworth, a grovelling man seeking mercy where it was not to be found. The Germans were very much on the wrong wavelength when trying to infiltrate radio spies into Britain.

10   The Spy Who
Collected Dolls

On a bright June morning in 1942 Mary Wallace, a maiden
lady living in Springfield, Ohio, was a very puzzled person
as she collected a letter left by the postman with the day's
mail. For one thing it was not addressed to her. It was
addressed to Señora Inez Lopez de Molinali, 2563 O'Higgins
C., Buenos Aires, Argentina. But in blue franking ink the
front of the envelope had been stamped 'Unknown at this
address – return to sender.'

On the reverse was the sender's name and address. Miss
Wallace stared at the words with a feeling of shock. They
read: 'Miss Mary Wallace, 1808 E. High Street, Springfield,
Ohio.' She studied the stamps and the circles over them and
learned that the redirected letter had been sent back from
Buenos Aires, to arrive in New York, where the letter had
been stamped again 'Grand Central Station'. In all a much-
travelled letter, produced by a neat typewriter, but she had
not sent it. Not unnaturally she felt she was entitled to know
the contents of a letter supposedly sent to Señora Molinali by
herself.

She slit the envelope and removed from it a sheet of
notepaper covered with typed words beginning 'Dear Friend'
and ending with her own signature, Mary Wallace. The date
on the letter was 20 May 1942. It had been sent by airmail.
The letter was as follows:

'Dear Friend,
You probably wonder what has become of me as I

haven't written to you for so long. We have had a pretty bad month or so. My little nephew, the one I adore so, had a malignant tumour on the brain and isn't expected to live, so we're all so crushed that we don't know what we are doing. They are giving him ex-ray on the head and they hope to check it, but give us absolutely no hope in a complete cure and maybe not even any relief. I am completely crushed.

You asked me to tell you about my collection a month ago. I had to give a talk to an art club so I talked about my dolls and figurines. The only new dolls I have are three lovely Irish dolls. One of these three dolls is an old fisherman with a net over his back, another is an old woman with wood on her back, and the third is a little boy.

Everyone seemed to enjoy my talk. I can only think of our sick boy these days.

You wrote me that you had sent a letter to Mr Shaw. He destroyed your letter. You know he has been ill. His car was damaged, but is being repaired now. I saw a few of his family about. They all say Mr Shaw will be back to work soon.

I do hope my letter is not too sad. There is not much I can write to you these days.

I came on this short trip for Mother on business before I make out her income tax report. That is also why I am learning to type.

Everyone seems busy these days. The streets are full of people.

Remember me to your family. Sorry I haven't written to you for long.

Truly
Mary Wallace

PS Mother wanted to go to Louville, but due to our worry the Louville plan put out our minds now.'

To Mary Wallace the letter read like gibberish except for one alarming fact. She did have a small nephew who suffered from a brain disease. One other fact was half true. She certainly had a collection of dolls and she had lectured to a club in Springfield – but she had no Irish dolls in her collection. So someone who had written the letter had known facts about her life and had used them in the body of a letter that for the most part read incoherently. That same someone had also produced a very fair imitation of her signature. Her first impulse was to tear up the offending letter. Then she changed her mind. She would let the local postmaster deal with it. After all, misuse of the mails in any way was his business.

When she took the letter to the Springfield postmaster and explained why it was puzzling he decided that he had best get in touch with the FBI. Mary Wallace did not have to wait long before she received a visit from a special agent. The Hoover man listened while she explained about her doll collection and her sick nephew.

'What about this Mr Shaw?' he asked.
'I don't know anyone of that name,' she informed him.
'You have no Irish dolls in your collection?'
'None. And something else is curious. I have no typewriter and I can't type. But I grant you that the signature resembles mine.'
'So someone unknown to you knows quite a deal about you, Miss Wallace.'
She nodded, and then said hesitantly, 'There is one other point. I do have three dolls that I bought recently in a doll shop in New York. But they are certainly not Irish dolls.'
'I'd like to see them.'

He was shown Miss Wallace's splendid collection of dolls, and her three latest acquisitions were pointed out. One was a fisherman, one an old woman with a bundle of wood, and the third was a little boy. 'But they are not Irish dolls,' she insisted.

When the FBI man asked her the address of the doll shop in New York he was given it at once. Miss Wallace did not have to look it up. After he had written it down he said,

'You've remembered the address of the doll shop.'

'Yes,' she said. 'I've written several times to the woman who runs it about particular dolls I wanted. I suppose you could say I'm a good customer.'

'What's the name of the woman who owns the shop?'

'Mrs Dickinson.'

'And you've met her?'

'Oh, yes, when I bought these three new dolls.'

'Then she knows that you have them?'

'She helped me select them. She seems to be an expert on dolls of all kinds, some very expensive indeed, some quite cheap.'

When the special agent left the house in East High Street he was certain that in some way a spy ring had blundered. His chiefs in Washington agreed with him. Particularly in the matter of the incoherent letter, which they decided had not been written by an uneducated person or someone with limited mental powers. That letter, they were convinced, had been specially contrived, and for only one purpose. To convey information, and to conceal the fact that the information was secret.

The FBI made contact with Navy Intelligence. Two interesting pieces of information were passed back. The US Navy had a cruiser named *Louisville* and a destroyer named *Shaw*. The possibility of coincidence in the employment of these names in the letter, even with one purposely misspelled, was ruled out. Someone was sending information secretly to the enemy.

In the summer of 1942 the USA was at war with Germany and Japan. To which of them had the message in the letter been sent? Mrs Dickinson was immediately suspect. She was checked, but nothing could be proved against her loyalty. Her doll shop at 718 Madison Avenue, New York, was put under constant observation. Mrs Velvalee Dickinson herself did nothing openly suspicious. She bought and sold dolls and the business of the shop seemed to take up all her time. She was dedicated to the collecting of dolls.

So began a waiting game. It continued, it seems somewhat surprisingly, for a year and a half, with American counter-espionage biding its time. In this interval the Americans became firmly convinced that the original letter dropped through the letter-box in East High Street, Springfield, had been intended for the Japanese. They based this argument on, first, the USS *Shaw* having been badly damaged at Pearl Harbour, and having been repaired and provided with a new bow structure in a shipyard in Honolulu; and, second, the USS *Louisville* having continued at sea for an extended period with her immediate whereabouts a top secret. From this they tried to decide the significance of the three so-called Irish dolls. The fisherman with his net could have been an aircraft carrier screened with a safety net, the old woman with the wood on her back could signify a warship with a wooden superstructure employed as camouflage, while the small boy could represent a smaller warship such as a destroyer.

The theory was passed to the postal censorship. At first they laughed, then they had second thoughts and became very co-operative. Finally they convinced themselves when they stopped a letter which mentioned dolls. The letter was supposedly sent by a woman in Portland, Oregon, to that same Señora Molinali who resided in a street named for an Argentine general with an Irish name. The really interesting part of the letter said:

'I just secured a lovely Siamese temple dancer. It had been damaged, that is tore in the middle. But it is now repaired and I like it very much. I could not get a mate for this Siamese dancer, so I am redressing just a small plain ordinary doll into a second Siam doll.'

The letter was directed via Naval Intelligence to the FBI and its famous forensic laboratory, which decided the letter had been contrived by the Mary Wallace letter's writer. The common clue was 'dolls', which was accepted to refer to warships. Eventually it was established that this passage supposedly from someone in Oregon meant that the writer had information about an aircraft carrier which had received a torpedo amidships. but had since been repaired. A second aircraft carrier had not been provided and accordingly a

120

warship was being converted into an aircraft carrier. Back went the reading to Naval Intelligence, who began checking the date of the letter in relation to the movement of aircraft carriers. A few days before the Oregon letter was written the USS *Saratoga* had left Puget Sound for the California naval base at San Diego.

Inquiries were made by US secret agents in Buenos Aires at the address of Señora Molinali. They learned that a man who had resided there had left. He had had airmail letters from the United States passed on to him. But when he had moved his US mail had been returned.

Before this was established conclusively another letter about dolls arrived at the home of Señora Molinali. But already the American postal censors had recorded its contents and the name and address of the person to whom it was to be returned in the event of non-delivery. She turned out to be a woman who claimed no knowledge of the letter.

'Do you know a Mrs Velvalee Dickinson?' an FBI man asked her casually.

The reply was anything but casual.

'Do I know her! I ordered some dolls from her, and because I haven't had time to send her a cheque she's been hounding me, and some of her letters are pretty offensive, I can tell you.'

When the Federal agent left the woman was still fuming against Velvalee Dickinson, one of whose 'offensive' letters was in the agent's pocket. The FBI forensic laboratory proved that it had been typed on the same machine that had typed the letters to Señora Molinali. A circle had been completed. Moreover, US Intelligence was suddenly aware that it knew something still unknown to the spy in Madison Avenue who used blue-printed letterheads on business paper, reading 'Velvalee Dickinson. Dolls – Antique – Foreign – Regional.'

The information gathered about the doll woman's background was now gone over again for a possible clue, hitherto unsuspected. She was an educated woman, born in Sacramento, who had attended Stanford University, and she claimed distant relationship with that Marshal Blücher who arrived at Waterloo after Wellington had won the battle. Her name before marriage was Malvena Blücher. She had no prison record, but her husband had been a very sick man in his last years and medical costs had been high. She had found the money. How was not known, and it seemed unlikely that she would have earned sufficient as a bank clerk or in her employ with the California Fruit Growers' Association.

Her husband had rented an office in the same building in San Francisco that housed the German and Japanese consulates. For a time they lived their private lives in the district known as Imperial Valley. It was the local Japanese colony. Velvalee Dickinson had joined for a time the American-Japanese Society, and was a member when she changed her job and joined an outfit handling the investment accounts of various Japanese with American nationality. But numbered among the firm's clients were some Japanese naval officers.

Then came the husband's illness requiring costly treatment. After his death she left California. That was in 1937. She went to New York and during the Christmas rush in that year she found a job in the department selling dolls at a well-known store. Her remuneration could have been only modest, but in 1938 she opened her own doll shop in Madison Avenue. Almost immediately her living standards changed. Money flowed in a fairly steady stream across her well-polished counters. She began with pricey dolls. Fifty dollars was the minimum price. Antique dolls of the Colonial period were ticketed as high as five hundred dollars. She did not sell dolls for children. All her stock in this period was for connoisseurs and the arty-crafty trade. Several Hollywood personalities and film stars patronized the Madison Avenue shop with blue letterheads on its notepaper.

Then, with cash in the bank, she expanded. She added porcelain figurines to the collection of antique dolls. Once well established she began to collect folk dolls from all over the world. After the native dolls from the South Seas and the Far East came carved animals and pottery pieces and some dolls one could give to an appreciative child.

The neat little woman with the square Teutonic face and very ready smile for anyone entering from the street did not look her fifty years. Behind the spectacles she wore her alert eyes were very observant and immensely alive. Invariably she stared up at a customer, which gave her a pert look, with her chin thrusting forward. She had to lift her chin when she conversed with anyone. She was under five feet tall.

There was a great deal of detail in the Intelligence compilation on Velvalee Dickinson, but nothing that was a real clue. The association with Japanese some years before the war did not point to intent to betray her country. It merely suggested she had an opportunity to make contacts that were later exploited.

The waiting game continued, not only letters being caught in the net of the postal censorship, but boxes containing dolls packaged and dispatched from Madison Avenue were held for discreet examination. Tucked under some of the boxed dolls were little notes that could have been innocent or, on the other hand, an important message containing information that had been coded. So the experts on codes and ciphers worked late trying to make something significant of doll chat that on the surface was no more than a friendly vendor's trade gossip.

But if the Intelligence groups interested in Velvalee Dickinson and the woman's doll shop in Madison Avenue continued their probing and investigating with a feeling of acute frustration, Velvalee Dickinson herself was not having a very comfortable time.

There were too many people calling at the shop and inspecting the stock she had on display. They were persons, men and women alike, who pretended to an interest in her high-priced wares, but a few questions left her convinced that they knew nothing about what they were handling. Most of them could not tell the difference between a Welsh doll with a steepled black hat, designed strictly for the summer tourist trade, and a French doll of the Louis XVI period that was worthy of a place in a private museum.

The little woman became, in her turn, suspicious and alerted by the interest these ignorant strangers were taking in her store. She decided she should absent herself for a time from New York. She had an assistant named Alma who was quite capable of taking charge in her absence.

She made her arrangements hurriedly, left Alma with enough cash to carry on, sent a hurried note to her mother, and then took a taxi. Before it had left Madison Avenue she had a feeling that she was being followed. She ordered the driver to change direction and take her to a large department store. From there she moved up and down in lifts until she was sure she had shaken off any pursuer, and only then did she make her way to Pennsylvania Station. But she took no chance. She boarded a train for Philadelphia without stopping to purchase a ticket. She bought one from the train's conductor. From Philadelphia she continued to Chicago, and from the Windy City to Portland, where she hurried to a Chinese restaurant. It was where a man who was a valuable contact was employed in a cover job. Hanging in the window was a one-word notice 'Closed'. Peering beyond the notice she saw the bare floor of a restaurant that had been vacated. Yet she had not been told. She knew that her contact must have been rounded up by Government agents. Did they have anything that spelled out her own complicity in a spy ring or were they just guessing because something had made them take a long hard look at her shop? She had to be sure.

After spending some time trying to contact other intermediaries who were no longer available to her she returned to New York. Almost the first thing she did was call at the bank where she rented a deposit box kept in the bank's vault. She went into the vault and opened her deposit box, which contained nearly twenty thousand dollars in cash. She might have been on the point of removing it preparatory to disappearing, but before she could close the deposit box and lock it she was suddenly no longer alone.

She stared at the two strangers. One flapped open a wallet, showing a gold badge. He said, 'We are agents of the Federal Bureau of Investigation. You are under arrest, Mrs. Dickinson.' Before he had finished speaking she had tried to crowd past his companion, who stopped her. Then she was struggling and clawing to free herself. But without success.

While she was held her premises were searched. She had forty thousand dollars in a secret cache. An interesting sum of money. That was the amount she owed the US Government in unpaid taxes. Clearly she did not believe in giving money readily to a Government she was helping to destroy.

She was arrested in January and kept in a women's detention prison for six months. Shortly before she was brought to trial on 27 July 1944, she tried to throw the blame for her involvement with the Japanese Secret Service on her husband who had died seven years before. She claimed that he had worked with the Japanese, and that she had been dragged into the aftermath of his manoeuvres. Her plea did not prevent her appearance in court before Judge Shackelford Miller, and she heard the US Attorney who was prosecuting outline the case against her.

'We are ready to prove that when the Japanese hired her,' he stated, 'they were hiring an old friend. It may be true that her husband, Lee Dickinson, was also at one time employed by Japan. But he died before Pearl Harbour. It is Velvalee, and not the late Lee Dickinson, who admits forging her customers' names to these letters. She claims her late husband is the guilty one and that she is innocent. But I charge that at least ten days before Pearl Harbour she had definite information that the Japanese were planning to go to war with this country.'

The prosecutor was interrupted by the prisoner's counsel, who made an appeal to the judge against this indictment, but he was overruled.

'What the defendant did,' continued the prosecution, 'was unspeakably foul. It is so horrible that one finds it difficult to believe that a native-born American, no matter how degraded and low, could be guilty of such acts.'

The acts referred to could have meant that she would be the first American woman to be found guilty of espionage in wartime, thereby earning a sentence of death. 'The dolls talked,' said the prosecutor, 'and we finally learned to understand their language.' But the evidence the prosecution was ready to submit was very largely circumstantial, claimed the defence after the Mary Wallace letter had been read to an attentive court. The prosecution countered with a claim that the coded information was vital to the enemies of the United States.

This was the most tense moment of the trial. The defence attorney asked for time to consult his client, who sat pale and shaking at his table, aware that the prosecution had four other letters they were prepared to submit as additional evidence. A consultation was granted, and within minutes the defence counsel told the court that his client was now ready to plead guilty provided the charges against her were changed – in effect, made less than treason. After further delay the court agreed, thus avoiding a long-drawn-out trial. Velvalee Dickinson had also, by her changed plea, avoided the possibility of being sentenced to death.

She was now, in substance, pleading guilty to avoiding and circumnavigating the wartime postal censorship. She went back to a prison cell to wait out the long hot summer days in dreadful loneliness until 15 August, the date when she would reappear before Judge Shackelford Miller to hear her sentence.

On that day she was asked if she had anything to say. She had indeed. Again she pushed the blame on the shoulders of her dead husband: 'It is he who agreed to work for Japan. They paid him twenty-five thousand dollars for his services. But I am innocent!'. In case that sounded incredible after the changed plea, she claimed that anything conveyed in her letters was of no real value to the Japanese. In fact, she had deliberately avoided giving any information which could directly endanger the safety of the United States.

It did not sound convincing, however, and the judge made this clear when he said sternly in his address to the prisoner,

'It is hard to believe that some people do not realize that our nation is engaged in a life-and-death struggle, and any help given to the enemy means the death of American boys who are fighting for our national security. You are a

126

natural-born citizen, with a university education. Yet you sold out to the Japanese. You were certainly engaged in espionage.'

He stared hard at the flinching woman and added, 'The indictment to which you have pleaded guilty is a serious matter. It borders close to treason.'

He went out of his way to underline this when he told her, 'You are fortunate that the Government did not have you tried on espionage charges.'

This was a reference to her being allowed to change her plea.

The penalty for such a conviction would have been death or life imprisonment.'

He sentenced her to ten years in prison. Velvalee Dickinson broke down and wept. Then she was led away to jail and eventual obscurity, a dejected and discredited woman who had been an expert on the subject of dolls, but a spy who had failed, though she had come perilously close to achieving a notable success.

Two factors brought her little world of subterfuge and espionage tumbling about her slim shoulders. Someone in Argentina had neglected to notify her that a Japanese agent had been removed, and someone else in American Intelligence had shrewdly come to the right conclusion about the Mary Wallace letter and the hidden reference to warships when dolls were mentioned.

11 The Dead Man Told a Tale

Incredible though it may sound, of all the numerous spies operating on both sides in the Second World War, one of the most successful was a dead man. As a secret operation the whole affair of the dead man who was kitted out to tell a tale that was false was a complete success. It was planned simply and brilliantly. It went off without a hitch, and the dead man played his part to perfection. The whole point of the operation was deliberately to deceive the German General Staff at a crucial moment in time.

The year was 1943. The hostilities on two major fronts had swung away from favouring the Axis Powers, and it was suddenly vital to deceive the Germans about Allied intentions in Europe. The North African campaign had ended in victory. Italy was dangling like a rotten fruit from the Axis bough, ready to fall out of the war. The big question in Europe was when and where would the much-debated Second Front, for which the Soviet Army commanders were clamouring, open to force the Germans to fight on two fronts on the European mainland.

Intelligence officers attached to General Eisenhower's headquarters 'somewhere in England' strove to find a method and a practical scheme by which the Germans could be fed misleading information that would be accepted at face value because it was both startlingly unexpected and utterly convincing.

As theoretical strategy the notion could not be faulted, but the tactical employment of the strategy was a vastly different

128

matter. A number of suggestions made by experienced Intelligence officers from each of the Services were considered
closely in detail and rejected for various practical operational
reasons. Then a British naval officer came up with an idea
that was breathtaking, challenging to the rigid military
mind, and quite impudent in conception. It was also
unquestionably macabre.

The officer who had the bizarre idea for fooling the Germans and using a dead man as a spy was Lieutenant Commander Ewen Montagu. He was a man of original ideas with
a sharp mind, a man capable of seeing clearly the implica-
tions of his own decisions. When he conceived the idea of the
dead-man spy he was aware that it sounded like something
taken from a sensational novel, but that in no way deterred
him from believing in it. Indeed, the qualities of being both
sensational and novel were those he sought. Only a conception having both those qualities could be expected to fool the
well-trained minds working for German Intelligence.

The idea meant using a 'planted' officer. One with
background and rank that would justify his being in possession of important dispatches. The trouble with this idea,
which was not by any means new, and was one recorded on
much-thumbed plans in a good many military archives
labelled secret, was that the captured decoy might well be
broken and forced to confess when in the hands of such a
brutal interrogation machine as the Gestapo. But a dead
man could not confess to the truth. Indeed, in life he would
never have known it.

This meant that his eventual captors would have to
depend on the sole evidence of their own eyes. They would
have to make their minds up on the basis of understanding
correctly the value of what they had found. Put simply, it
would be a brilliant trick, worthy of an experienced con
man. For that was what would be done, in effect. The
Germans would be conned.

When eventually the idea filtered upwards to executive
staff level there were some shocked and sceptical listeners.
Objections were raised, but these were more emotional than
valid on purely military grounds. The more the outline of the

idea was considered, the more it was appreciated that, if the scheme could be operated, it had more chance of succeeding than any other that had been put forward. The objections were overruled. Both military and Intelligence thinking became positive instead of negative. The go-ahead order was given. Then the search was on to find a suitable subject.

It was not anticipated that finding that suitable subject would be easy. In the meantime some shrewd minds were put to the task of working out precisely how the subject would be used. Again a number of suggestions were considered in depth and discounted for practical reasons, until eventually the one generally supported and agreed upon was defined.

The subject chosen would be dressed in an officer's uniform, that of an officer in the Royal Marines. Everything would be done to provide him with the appearance of an official courier carrying important dispatches. These would be locked in an official courier's dispatch case, which would be attached to the body by a length of slim chain. From the steel circle around the body the end of the chain would continue down one arm, under the jacket's sleeve, so as to leave the handle of the dispatch case positioned for comfortable holding by the courier's right hand.

The contents of the dispatch case were most carefully worked out, for after the body had been brought to the notice of the enemy, preferably by a citizen of a neutral country, to add to the overall realism and credibility of the plan, it would be the 'official' papers in the dispatch case that would work the confidence trick.

Such a courier would normally be carrying more than one top-secret dispatch. Accordingly a number of such documents had to be devised, each distinct but all supporting the information that would be hailed by the German discoverers as a breakthrough of Allied intentions about the Second Front, which was being debated and argued in newspapers and parliaments alike and about which sundry politicians were waxing fervidly and angrily, with every intention of pressuring the High Command in Britain to start a fresh invasion of the European mainland.

The Germans were known to be anxious to come by any hint or pointer that would indicate when the Second Front would become a reality. They had numerous divisions waiting poised in the south of France, many others behind the chain of fortifications they had built along the Channel coast. Those divisions were trained to repel invaders from the sea. It was important that their numbers should be reduced in areas where an Anglo-American invasion force eventually landed. To ensure this the Germans had to be induced to move some of their divisions to other regions, preferably at a maximum distance from the intended invasion coast.

Therefore the various fictional dispatches were carefully contrived to produce information that could be deduced by trained military minds. Nothing had to be put down in the dispatches that was too obvious. But naturally the key to the whole deception would be in one dispatch which would alert the Intelligence men reading through the contents of the dispatch case. All dispatches would be sealed in waterproof envelopes. This was essential, for the dead-man carrier was to arrive at his destination from the sea. It was intended that the dead man, with personal papers stating a created identity that could be checked by German Intelligence, would be cast adrift at a place where the local tides would be certain to carry the supposed courier with his chained dispatch case towards a neutral shore. The body would be recovered, and it would not be long before German Intelligence was alerted.

So the dispatches were prepared and sealed in their special waterproof envelopes. One of them was an acknowledgement of instructions received to prepare an invasion plan to be directed at the south of France. The Allies who had driven the Germans and Italians out of North Africa and ended disastrously the historic mission of General Rommel with his Afrika Korps would be seen, through this dispatch and the others, to be geared for crow-hopping northward across the Mediterranean towards Sardinia, and from this island of the mysterious Nuraghi the invasion of southern France would be mounted.

On paper such a move was logical and more or less direct. Moreover, it would be a move that could be seen by alert

Intelligence men as a natural projection of the invasion of Sicily and the Italian mainland. However, there was a passage specially inserted in the most informative of the dispatches that actually referred to Sicily as being the place from which the taking of Sardinia, the first real step, would be mounted. This point was deemed to hold special significance because it must appear a natural focussing place for a vital supply base. Other details in the phony dispatches would relate to minor matters which had significance at the time the dead man was cast adrift. Dates were carefully checked, names verified, and even some military units which were on the move to other places were referred to in their old positions, which were known to the Germans. The dispatches, in short, would be most convincing. Also, they would be alarming. Primarily because they would tell of something the Germans were expecting.

The next step was to decide on what personal papers the courier should carry. Letters from home and family, cheque-book, military papers, even evidence that the courier had been in London recently on leave. It was also essential to establish that he had been drowned as the result of an accident. The best suggestion was to make him a passenger in an aircraft that had been brought down in the Bay of Biscay. A fair number of such aircraft were lost between Gibraltar and the English Channel. It would be impossible for the Germans to check which. What would be convincing, apart from the alleged facts provided by the contents of the dead man's pockets and his dispatch case, would be the way he was found.

It was intended that the body should be cast adrift from a submarine at a known fishing ground in the Bay of Biscay used by Spanish fishermen. They would sight the bobbing body in the waves and one of them would certainly haul it inboard. Spain was a neutral country not unfriendly to the Germans, who had actively supported General Franco during the Spanish Civil War. Word that the body of a British courier had been recovered from the sea would reach German Intelligence within a very short time of a fishing boat's crew landing and reporting to the local police. The mere fact that the body had been recovered by Spanish nationals would dispel any first-held suspicions of the Germans. It would seem that the Spanish Government was bending backward to be friendly.

When final approval was given to the prepared plan a few refinements were added as psychologically convincing. The courier would be carrying British dispatches and these would be sent from one high-ranking officer to another. Such officers could be expected to be on close personal terms with each other, and it would be not inconsistent with their character for some off-the-record comments to be included in the dispatches. So one contained a critical observation on the Americans' apparent readiness to hand out medals of all kinds so that an army uniform could have the left breast smeared with a grotesque display of pieces of colourful ribbon. Even the Americans had a name for such a peacock display. They referred to it as 'lettuce'.

The fact that such personal comments would be found in the locked dispatch case would tell the Germans that feeling could grate badly between allies. Any German Intelligence officer would find this natural, acceptable, and therefore convincing. It was another detail that might be expected by a shrewd and analytical mind.

After some top-brass debate it was finally agreed that the dispatch intended to leak the invasion plan would be signed by the deputy chief of the British Imperial General Staff. It would be addressed to General Sir Harold Alexander, who had been Montgomery's superior in North Africa, and was currently the commanding officer of the Eighteenth Army Group under General Eisenhower. Such a dispatch would appear to the Germans like a gift from their own special gods in Valhalla.

However, with the details of what was to be found on the dead man settled, it became a matter of urgency to find a suitable subject for this curious but vitally important role.

No ordinary victim of heart attack or similar disease would be eligible, for it was certain that the Germans would have expert pathologists working on the corpse taken from the sea. There could be no question of chancing their discovery of a cause of death not in keeping with the dead man's role.

The chosen corpse had to be that of a man young enough to be the officer described in his personal papers. He could not be the victim of an accident because this would most likely injure the body in ways that would arouse suspicion. He must not be an outdoor type who worked with his hands or a craftsman who bore the marks of his trade.

One way of obtaining the body was firmly ruled out. There was to be no secret robbing of a graveyard. The most likely chance of obtaining a suitable dead man was to apply to a hospital where a man who fitted the part had recently died. But this meant involving his relatives. If their consent was not given readily there was to be no attempt to coerce them into changing their minds.

The operation of finding the required dead man was fraught with a large number of difficulties, all of which had to be overcome before the formal go-ahead could be granted those who would prepare the dead man for his incredible mission. After a great deal of inquiry a hospital fatality was reported and the dead man was found to have a medical history that would be acceptable to any pathologist holding a post-mortem and submitting his findings to Military Intelligence. The dead man's next of kin were approached. At first they seemed aghast, as was expected, that the dead man should be used in this incredible fashion. But they were told the reasons in broad outline and it was explained to them how the dead man would posthumously be performing a rare act of patriotism. Was their own patriotism equal to the demand being made on it?

Fortunately for the anxious group working with Ewen Montagu it was. But they had one reservation. 'Can you assure us,' they wanted to know, 'that the body will not be desecrated?' The idea that it might be was held in repugnance. They were assured that the Spanish authorities, after the body had been retrieved from the sea, would almost certainly undertake to arrange an interment with full military honours. This reply and assurance relieved the anxiety they felt. They gave their consent with no reservation.

So finally there was nothing to prevent the last stage of

actually creating the bogus Major William Martin, RM, who would later be found to have died of pneumonia, which was perfect, for the disease could have been brought on by immersion in the cold waters of the Bay of Biscay. This was checked with several British pathologists, each of whom agreed that the pulmonary fluid that would subsequently be discovered during a post-mortem would be medically convincing.

Now came the business of filling in the bogus major's background. Because he had died at a young age he was provided with a sweetheart as bogus as himself. A letter from her was prepared and placed among the other personal possessions he was to carry. It was written in endearing terms and referred to their recent engagement. A Bond Street jeweller who was known internationally was approached. He provided an authentic receipt for the cash received for a suitable engagement ring, and this was dated to comply with the terms in the letter from the fictitious sweetheart.

To correspond with the period Major Martin was allegedly on leave to become engaged, another dated receipt was included in his personal papers. This one was for his bill for room and meals in an officer's hostel in London. Such a man, however, would have a family interested in his welfare. A letter from Martin Senior held notes of anxiety about his son's welfare, especially as he had been made into a sort of King's Messenger, asked after his health, offered scraps of home news, and ended with a parental injunction to take care of himself.

The plan was for Major Martin to move into history on a night in spring. The month was April, one when poets become nostalgic. The raids on London had developed a lull, so it was without any death-dealing fanfare for the latest concept in spies that the corpse dressed in the uniform of a Royal Marines major was loaded into an inconspicuous van late at night. The most secret group in England travelled north through the hours of darkness. It was an eerie sensation, to be seated in that van and listening to the rattling of the metal cylinder containing Major Martin each time the van's wheels encountered a bump or pothole in the road, for that cylinder, which weighed several hundred pounds, was packed with dry ice. The major who had been created by back-room Service types was virtually in a deep freeze while speeding to his rendezvous with a posthumous destiny.

The van arrived at a Northern submarine base shortly after daylight. The submarine *Seraph* was waiting to receive the strangest passenger to board a submarine. The shiny metal cylinder was carried aboard HMS *Seraph* and stowed in a cabin specially prepared to receive the Royal Marines major. The van was parked some distance from the submarine dock and a conference was held on board the *Seraph*. Charts were spread out on a wardroom table. Tables of currents were consulted. Meteorological forecasts were checked. It was the final briefing with the commander of the *Seraph* before the submarine sailed for the seas off the Spanish port of Huelva, north of Cadiz and the sherry capital of Jerez de la Frontera. That was where Major Martin was to perform.

If Drake could be said to have singed a king's beard off Cadiz, then the frozen major was about to fool the Nazi General Staff in the same historic area. Indeed, he was about to give certain high-ranking *Wehrmacht* officers quite an expensive tonsorial treatment. Moreover, his posthumous appearance on a world stage would be a performance that would save countless lives of the Anglo-American forces shortly to be committed to a death struggle for victory in Europe.

It was a dark night when the *Seraph* surfaced not far off the Spanish coast. The ice-packed metal cylinder with its uniformed occupant, the dispatch case held in now rigid fingers, was removed from the cabin and taken on deck. It was opened. The ice packing was still crisp and very cold. Major Martin was removed, his uniform covered with a glistening artificial hoar frost. However, in those latitudes in the spring of the year frost would not survive for more than a few minutes. Even as the handlers removed the body some of the frost was vanishing, soaking the dark uniform. The submarine's medical officer hurriedly examined the body and pronounced it in a satisfactory state.

No further time was lost. Major Martin, R M, was lowered over the *Seraph*'s side and he went down into the sea. The captain of the submarine saluted. Eyes strained to see the bobbing body that would very soon begin to thaw out now it was immersed in salt water. Major Martin vanished.

A sharp word of command was given, and the *Seraph* moved from that secret burial place, engines in reverse, to avoid the propellers dragging the body in their wake. The effect of the propellers' wash had been calculated in conjunction with the tide running at that moment and the whip of a fairly strong breeze. The time was four-thirty.

Well clear of where Major Martin's body would be tossing in the swell, the *Seraph*'s engine room received instructions to move ahead. As the submarine turned into the wind a rubber dinghy with a single paddle was brought up on deck. The *Seraph*'s head was turning when the dinghy, upside-down, was launched into the sea. The bright yellow patch of the overturned dinghy remained a diminishing blot on the grey-green sea as the submarine's engine telegraph rang a fresh instruction. Hatches were closed. *Seraph*, mission over, slipped under the waves before dawnlight could betray her presence to any other ocean prowler.

The voyage back to base was as uneventful as the journey out. The submarine's return was signalled to the Admiralty. Naval Intelligence saw that the British naval attaché at the embassy in Lisbon was alerted. He was to send word of any happening in the Iberian peninsular that suggested Major Martin had been taken ashore and been examined by German Intelligence.

As things worked out, that important word from Lisbon was not long delayed. The Spanish Government's marine department sent the British naval attaché the information that fishermen operating in the wide bay to the south-west of Huelva had recovered the body of a British officer. He was, from his personal papers, a certain William Martin, who had been a major in the Royal Marines. The body had been buried with full military honours. There was no word of the dead man being a courier in possession of a dispatch case with top-secret papers. It would seem that the Spanish felt they had something to keep quiet about. This produced wry but appreciative smiles in London.

Another signal was sent to Lisbon. It was explained to the British naval attaché that Major Martin had been a special courier at the time of his loss at sea. He should have had important and vital dispatches with him. The man in Lisbon was requested to instigate the most cautious inquiries to establish whether the Spanish authorities had recovered the dispatch case and its contents. If there was no satisfactory outcome to these inquiries, then further inquiries were to be made in the region where the fishermen had landed the body. Should an opportunity arise he was to obtain the dispatch case and send it to London without delay. The attaché was at no stage informed of the full story behind the finding of a Royal Marines major's body and the reason for this follow-up inquiry. He used his contacts and before long the Government in Madrid knew that he was seeking the dispatch case. Word was sent to him by a roundabout diplomatic way that the dispatch case was in the custody of the Spanish authorities and would be released shortly. News of this was sent to the men waiting in London.

They did not have to wait very long. The dispatch case arrived in Lisbon and was sent on by the attaché to London, where those really interested in examining it passed it to experts, who eventually reported back to Intelligence that the case had been tampered with and certainly unlocked. Moreover, the contents had been cleverly opened and the waterproof letters resealed with great pains, so that a hurried glance would reveal no sign of them having been induced to reveal their secret contents. This meant that the decoy had been accepted at face value and the dispatches were no longer a secret unshared with German Intelligence. Whether German Intelligence was tricked or not was eventually made very manifest.

It is history that Field Marshal Keitel, the German Supreme Commander, gave his Staff an urgent order. They prepared new plans and new dispositions for many of the divisions under Keitel's command. All across Europe German soldiers and *matériel* were suddenly on the move, heading for the Mediterranean to prevent a crow-hopping Allied landing in Sardinia preparatory to a full-scale invasion of the south of France.

By the time the deception was known the Anglo-American forces were forcing their way up the mountainous spine of Italy and many divisions that could have made their passage more difficult and certainly more costly in lives were hundreds of miles distant from where they could have been used effectively.

The German Military Intelligence, in fact, were so baffled and reluctant to give up the secret they felt they shared that some of those divisions were late in being sent northwards to the Normandy beaches and bocage after D day had dawned. Possibly this fact was contributory to General Patton's Third Army being able to sweep south and then east, meeting at times only light opposition. Major William Martin, RM, had achieved the most fantastic one-man *coup* of the war.

12 Special Correspondent –Very Special Spy

If the saga of Major Martin, RM, was the most unusual espionage drama of the Second World War, then that of Richard Sorge, the Soviets' man in Tokyo, was certainly the most successful. As a double agent he had his own quality of uniqueness. No man could keep a secret better. No man could judge better the intrinsic value of a secret.

He was established and vouched for in Tokyo by Major-General Eugen Ott, the German Ambassador to Japan before war was declared. Indeed, to General Ott he was a valued friend. He not only shared many of the secrets that became the ambassador's property, but he actively helped Ott to make decisions affecting the welfare of the Third Reich.

Yet one secret he did not share with the German ambassador. His grandfather had been secretary to Karl Marx. Sorge, German born, had served with the German Imperial Army in the First World War, in which he had been wounded three times. But after that war he had become disillusioned with the world he had known and turned to the Communism of Lenin and Trotsky. He had arrived in Russia, a man without a soul seeking a substitute he thought he had found. Perhaps he had, for he served the Communist world cause faithfully. Once the Foreign Intelligence service in Russia had come to realize the quality of this new recruit who had ancestral connections with Karl Marx he was swept up like a discarded paper bag in the path of a new broom.

He was sent to one of the newly established Soviet espionage schools, and there the disillusioned German soldier who had bled for his fatherland was turned into a dedicated servant of the Kremlin.

He developed marked aptitudes for the work of a secret agent, and his quality was first tested when he was sent to Shanghai, where his task was to organize a spy web and lay the foundations for further exploitation in China by other Communist cells. To help him he secured the services of Communists of other nations. They provided him with excellent cover and helped him build up a valuable reputation in the Far East as an international figure. He knew he was being used, but that was what he wanted: to help the Comintern prepare the ground for an eventual Communist take-over in China, which the Kremlin policy-makers believed would one day fall to the ambitions of Imperialist Japan, one of the victors of the First World War and a country determined upon expansion.

In the long term Sorge was intended to move on to Japan after completing his espionage groundwork operations in China. When he arrived in Japan history was already making new whirlpools in some very troubled waters. Japan was seemingly remote and outward-looking. Sorge's job was to dig into the country's vitals. To help and to guide him he was introduced to certain Soviet-accepted allies. Some of these were the most unlikely persons. They must have surprised even the very unflappable Sorge. Hozumi Ozaki was such a confederate and conspirator. He was a well-known scholar and journalist, accepted by the heirs of Bushido, and a person seemingly destined for power in the land of Nippon. Ozaki was a man who could keep a secret with the inscrutable composure of an Oriental. He was to open doors for Sorge that would otherwise have been kept locked. They were Marxist birds of deep-dyed plumage.

Another was a German who first joined Sorge in Shanghai. He was the man who held responsibility for Sorge's being at all times able to communicate with his superiors. He handled all radio messages and was a competent technician. Curiously he loved a woman named Anna who despised

Communists but returned the affection of bluff-mannered Max Klausen, who perspired easily and became red in the face when he drank too much. His drinking brought him censure from Moscow, which summoned him back for a stern dressing down. Anna went with him. Those were days when few brought home in disgrace returned to kick up their heels in a free society. Max Klausen was one of them. He went back to join Sorge, and Anna accompanied him. Sorge had already reported that, without Max Klausen, he was a man minus one arm.

In 1938 Sorge was badly injured when he crashed his motorcycle into a wall. While he lay covered with blood and moaning an ambulance arrived and he was taken to hospital, where he recovered consciousness just long enough to speak a few words. They were a name and a phone number. The hospital rang the number and told someone answering to the name what had happened. A short while later a thickset, rather worried-looking man arrived and insisted on seeing the accident case against the protests of the medical staff. After a glance at the unconscious Sorge's face the newcomer looked around for the patient's jacket, and when he found it removed from an inside pocket an envelope which was stained with blood. He slipped the envelope into his own pocket and told the nurse watching him with puzzled gaze, 'Take the best of care of him'. That man was Max Klausen.

Sorge recovered from his accident after the hospital staff had considered his chances slim. He went back to work setting up his spy cell, adding to its numbers a Yugoslav officer who had appeared in Japan as correspondent for a number of European newspapers. Another was a Japanese artist who had been living in the States and had tired of the American way of life.

Vital messages bearing valuable information about secret negotiations that were continuing between Japan and Nazi Germany were sent back to Moscow by Sorge. Unexpectedly he was summoned back to Moscow. Behind him he left Max Klausen in charge, his cover that of a salesman for a number of German exporting firms.

Arrived in Moscow, Sorge was interviewed by General

Beldin of the Red Army's Fourth Bureau, which handled overseas military espionage. They spent three months re-shuffling the entire cellular structure of the espionage network that had been set up by Sorge. Two main sections were arranged for independent operations, the China Unit and the Japan Unit, and yet at any given time they could be used to complement each other. The two men worked for the most part in an isolated country house, guarded day and night.

From what Sorge had already supplied Beldin it was certain that Germany and Japan were slowly coming together as allies. Sorge returned to Berlin, risking possible arrest for having been a known Communist in Hamburg after the First World War. Now he joined the Nazi Party. In Hamburg his Communist records disappeared mysteriously. Even the Gestapo accepted him. Next came the event that gave him open cover for returning to the Far East. The editor of the Frankfurt *Gazette* received a cordial letter from an American woman friend, Agnes Smedley, who was passing on information. If he required a good correspondent in Tokyo Dr Richard Sorge would be an excellent one. The Frankfurt editor wrote to Sorge in Berlin. Sorge did not seem at all keen to accept the assignment. He was persuaded, as the Frankfurt editor thought, by an offer of three times the normal salary for the post. Sorge was signed up and given a farewell dinner. One of the guests was Josef Goebbels.

So a new Richard Sorge arrived in Japan, the official correspondent for a well-known German newspaper. He was very soon persona grata with the Tokyo Press Club, and a man who had access to the German Ambassador. In fact, the leopard had not only changed its spots, but had learned to purr most disarmingly.

Just how deviously Sorge had planned with Beldin was proved at the meeting with Branko de Voukelitch, a correspondent for a French paper, but one of the men given special spy status in that country house outside Moscow. Sorge was studying a book at a Press conference when the sleek and smiling de Voukelitch came up to him.

'Dr Sorge, isn't it?'

143

Sorge looked up. 'Yes. You are de Voukelitch? We have met, I believe.'

It was all very smooth. The other looked over Sorge's shoulder and appeared interested in the book.

'I've read it, a good story I thought. I remember on page 128 there's a girl who is the kind that always fascinates me.'

Sorge looked up and shook his head. 'Surely you are mistaken. She doesn't appear until page 171.'

The French correspondent appeared surprised, but there was amusement in his eyes. The two Soviet agents had just exchanged code signals. Before they left the conference Sorge told the other to give a cocktail party for Press Club members and to invite Ozaki, who was back from Shanghai, and also the Japanese American artist Yotoko Miyagi, who had vanished from Los Angeles in mysterious circumstances, had been reported missing, and had been sought for weeks by the Los Angeles police, who decided he must have died in some accident.

When eventually Sorge met Miyagi the Japanese American was congratulated on the way he had vanished without trace. 'The best spies are "dead" spies,' Sorge is said to have remarked. He had no idea how literally true his words were to be taken by members of British Naval Intelligence, who had never heard them.

Before long Sorge had a five-man unit rearranged and functioning smoothly according to the agreement made with Beldin. When Beldin was told he sent a three-word secret message: 'Time is scarce.' Sorge rented a large house and invited fifty persons to a generous house-warming. Most of the guests were persons who held responsible positions in the Tokyo Government. At midnight six cars drew up outside the house. Out climbed some of the most fashionable geisha girls in the Japanese capital.

He upset the wives of European correspondents with this provision of feminine company, but he made friends he needed among the Japanese. The German Ambassador is said to have taken him to task for providing the geisha girls.

'It hardly becomes a responsible correspondent,' he is said to have told Sorge.

'But I like giving parties,' Sorge replied, in no way put out, 'and I think Tokyo will like them.'

Tokyo did. Sorge's parties, which became a cover for meeting many important contacts, became for a time the talk of the town. They were fashionable. They were also extremely popular because the drink never ceased from flowing. Indeed, quite a number of highly placed Japanese officials became intoxicated with Western hard liquor at those parties and talked indiscreetly off the record to Sorge and his other colleagues in the Soviet spy ring.

There was one other most useful cover provided by this series of parties that lasted into the small hours. While the merriment was most infectious Klausen was down in a basement tapping on a Morse keyboard. The messages were picked up in Moscow. Time, as Beldin had warned, was scarce. So the five spy chiefs of the Tokyo ring became specialists under their covers.

Sorge co-ordinated what could be learned directly from his own contacts like Ozaki, who had become a political correspondent with entrée into Government inner circles. Klausen, apart from providing the radio contacts for the group, covered the industrial scene and reported on such matters as the strategic materials being purchased in bulk by Japanese Government agencies. Miyagi specialized in army and navy matters, and had been fortunate to receive a commission to paint an admiral's wife in what was termed the American manner. The wives of many Service chiefs wanted him to make them modestly immortal with his competent brushwork, which had not been appreciated in Los Angeles. He indulged the afternoon chatterers sitting for their portraits and became accepted by their husbands. Among the Western embassies moved de Voukelitch, the sophisticated French correspondent of Yugoslav descent. He was the kind of man who had the manner and professional charm to inspire confidences to be passed on in exchange for a salty story.

One of the group's really important achievements was having Hozumi Ozaki made a personal assistant to the Japanese Prime Minister, Prince Konoye. All was progressing favourably, but Beldin was impatient. He sent another message in the urgent vein of the first. It arrived two months later. 'Time is a commodity we lack.'

Within days Ozaki brought Sorge news from Prince Konoye of the Japanese intention to invade China. It is said this was such a momentous piece of news that back to Tokyo came a message Klausen wrote down and gave to Sorge: 'Confirm. The Chief.' The Chief was Stalin. Richard Sorge had moved into the big time as a world spy.

By this time he was Tokyo correspondent for a whole group of newspapers. In addition to the *Frankfurter Zeitung* he was covering the Japanese scene for the *Burgen Kurrier,* the *Technische Rundschau,* and the *Amsterdam Handelsblatt.* So effective was his cover that for eight incredible years he operated in Tokyo without the Germans suspecting his real allegiance and without the Kempeitai, the Japanese counter-espionage group, which in its heyday had about seventy thousand members, being able to bare the truth about the man who ostensibly enjoyed parties and good times.

It was from Sorge that the Kremlin received the first intimation of the formation of the notorious Berlin-Rome-Tokyo Axis. Previously Sorge had reported the coming two-week mutiny of the younger elements in the Japanese armed forces. For those two weeks there had been bloody house-to-house fighting in Tokyo, and finally the Old Guard were worsted and succum-ed to the demands of the younger and more modern spirits imbued with revolutionary fervour. The Western powers had been caught by surprise: not the Kremlin as three weeks before the revolt Sorge had informed them through the Fourth Bureau, 'The junior and younger elements of the Japanese Army will take over from their older leaders by force. The uprising can be expected in the last days of February.'

He was certain of this information because Hozumi Ozaki was the man who pushed the Japanese Prime Minister into slowing up the Chinese war, to avoid an eventual confrontation with the Soviet on the Siberian border. If war was coming, it was better for the Kremlin to have Japan turn against the USA rather than the Soviet Union.

As it chanced Klausen's transmitter had been used so continuously at this period that it required a replacement. He took two months to build a much more powerful radio, and then the old one had to be jettisoned. It was agreed that it should be taken to a deep lake and dropped to the bottom. The lake chosen was Yamanaka, and on a summer day the group set out on a typical German hike, but were stopped by a Kempeitai officer, who wanted to know where they were headed. When they told him they were on a cross-country walk he pointed out that they were carrying heavy equipment.

'We have good appetites,' said Klausen, but it was a lame effort, and de Voukelitch did better.

'If you must know,' he told the suspicious Japanese, 'we're carrying a supply of good München beer. I suggest we sit down right now and have some.'

It was a bold bluff, and the man posing as a French correspondent was taking a chance, but one he considered reasonable, for Kempeitai officers were forbidden from drinking in the company of foreigners. The punishment for disobeying was grim. The culprit was strapped to a post and a flexible steel ring was screwed tighter and tighter until it was impossible to breathe. It was a form of garrotting peculiar to the Japanese military forces, shared between captured foreign spies and disobedient members of the Kempeitai.

On this occasion the Kempeitai officer was quick to refuse a drink and waved the party of hikers on their way. The discarded radio was a short time later at the bottom of the deep lake. When the others told Sorge of the incident he decided to halt all radio transmissions for a time, purely as a precaution. Within days he was sitting with General Ott in the German Embassy, where he reported that his paper had reason to believe military talks were continuing between

Berlin and Tokyo. Ott smiled and shrugged. 'I can tell you nothing,' he said.

A week later he had changed his mind, as though he had been instructed to confirm a confidential leak intended only for a Frankfurt editor's ears. 'A German-Japanese pact is currently being negotiated in Berlin,' he told Sorge. The radio silence was rescinded. Klausen tapped out the news to Moscow's listeners.

Sorge believed that Colonel Osaki of the Kempeitai might have learned in a roundabout way of the secret broadcasts, although he was unable to locate the transmitter. This was because the new transmitter did not relay a coded message twice from the same place. Klausen was kept on the move. But perhaps even more tricky to overcome was a Sorge device to make discovery virtually impossible. After each two hundred and fifty words the wavelength was changed. But what kept the colonel suspicious was that each time there was a major historical development involving Japan the number of the secret broadcasts increased. Often they were tripled.

Ott, who had become German Ambassador, did not help the Japanese by showing his trust in Sorge to the extent of making him the German Embassy's information officer. He met Sorge each morning over breakfast to discuss press releases for the day. Hans Otto Meissner, who was a secretary at the embassy at this time, later said of the breakfast parleys,

'Looking back, I am appalled when I think of the confidential documents the ambassador would not disclose to me or to any other German official, but which he freely showed to Sorge. Yet the ambassador had every reason for confidence. The entire staff, including myself, believed Sorge to be exactly what he appeared to be.'

His embassy task had a two-way traffic. Not only was he receiving confidential information from the Germans, but he began to be cultivated by influential Japanese who tried to get the man who had an image of being a *bon viveur* to share some of his information with them. Sorge used both for the advantage of his Kremlin masters. Largely due to his efforts the Japanese came to see the United States as their arch-enemy in place of the Soviet Union. But he encountered some risks that had to be run, as when he ordered de Voukelitch and Klausen to bring a short-wave transmitter to Tokyo from a house in the country. They travelled after dark, but were stopped by a Japanese policeman.

'Where are you going?' he asked brusquely.

Klausen left the other to explain: 'The Sennari Res-taurant,' said de Voukelitch, his hands firm on the satchel containing the transmitter.

The policeman snapped, 'Your left rear light is out. Get it fixed.'

That close shave made Sorge perspire freely. He forthwith rented a beach house and a boat. From that time forward broadcasts to Moscow would only be undertaken when the boat's sails were hoisted. Klausen was given implicit instructions to dump his equipment overboard if a Japanese Customs patrol boat approached.

But Sorge, perhaps deservedly when one considers his amazing bluff, was lucky upon occasion when luck was essential for him. Colonel Osaki still hunted the mysterious radio with coded messages his men could not break down. He approached Ambassador Ott, as an ally of Japan. Ott told Sorge of the spy hunt. A curious game of deadly deception began, with the Kempeitai colonel making no real progress because Sorge knew his moves in advance.

Then Sorge's cup was suddenly overflowing. On 1 May 1941, Hitler informed a startled Japanese Ambassador in Berlin that he was about to attack the Soviet Union. Within forty-eight hours Hozumi Ozaki attended a Cabinet meeting in Tokyo where the news was discussed. When the meeting broke up he drove to meet Sorge and told him the momen-tous news and the official Japanese line to be taken. This was an endorsement of the Nazis' opening an Eastern Front and marching into Russia, with Japan holding a reserved posi-tion in the matter of direct participation as an active ally of the Germans.

Sorge could not waste time, but he had to check the news. He did this at breakfast next day with General Ott, who was in a genial mood at the prospect of the *Wehrmacht* slicing through any Soviet resistance with their proved *Blitzkreig* techniques. Sorge had Klausen send this message to the Kremlin: 'One hundred and seventy German divisions will attack the Soviet Union along its entire western border on 2 June heading for Moscow.'

Four months later, when the Soviet Union had suffered severe casualties from the limited *Drang nach Osten* in compliance with a centuries-old German dream, Sorge sent another urgent message to the Kremlin. The date was 3 October and the message read: 'The Japanese are making ready for war in the Pacific, according to highest sources. They will not – I repeat they will not – at any time strike at the Soviet Union.' Pearl Harbour was two months away.

On the night of 19 October advance German units reached the outskirts of Moscow. Shortly afterwards a swastika flag fluttered from the roof of the building housing *Pravda*. It was the high-water mark of the German advance. Within twenty-four hours fresh Soviet troops were pouring into Moscow and the Germans were in retreat. Another of Stalin's brief messages to Sorge signed 'The Chief' was taken down by Klausen on his boat. It read: 'You saved our lives.' When Sorge read this he said something most peculiar and strange. It certainly shocked Klausen. 'I don't give a damn who wins the war,' Sorge said.

Such a sentiment ran completely counter to all he had contrived and done for eight incredibly fantastic years as double agent really working for the Kremlin. In that period he had used Klausen to transmit to Moscow some two hundred and fifty messages that had contained more than two hundred thousand separate word groups. In addition he had dispatched by special courier for collection in Shanghai a considerable number of film reports, including documents and pages photographed from secret volumes.

That same night after receiving Stalin's short message he sat in Tokyo's Fuji Club, watching the lovely Irish-Japanese performer Kiyomi. She in turn was watching him, for they had found a mutual attraction, which was why she saw a waiter now believed to have been a member of the Japan Unit drop a screwed-up piece of paper by Sorge's chair. He recovered it and for the next moments forgot Kiyomi as he read: 'Japanese carrier force will attack US Navy at Pearl Harbour probably at dawn December 6th, according to reliable Admiralty source.' That was the night of 21 October. Someone was providing Sorge with very advanced information about Japan's change from a reserved position to that of an active military partner of the Axis Powers.

When Kiyomi had finished her last appearance of the evening she drove with Sorge to the beach house. Before they arrived Sorge, who was suddenly nervous, became suspicious of a car he thought was trailing them. He took out a lighter to burn the screwed-up ball of paper with the message. But the lighter was out of fuel. He tore the message into small pieces and let them drift out of the window. He was silent on the rest of the journey to the beach house, where he left Kiyomi for a time while he joined Klausen on the boat. After the latest piece of hot news had been transmitted Sorge told his colleague,

'I'm disbanding the unit.'
'For heaven's sake why?' asked an amazed Klausen.
'I believe the Japanese police are following me and will soon overtake us,' Sorge said reflectively. 'All members of the unit must take immediate steps to avoid arrest. In any case, our real task here is now finished.'

Max Klausen gave him no argument. Sorge was the boss. He set Sorge ashore and then turned his boat towards the open sea. Sorge walked back to the house, unaware that Colonel Osaki had been pressuring the woman in whom he was interested. She had phoned the colonel to tell him about the pieces of torn paper that had been thrown away. Osaki asked for a description of the locality.

The first real move to liquidate the Kremlin's Japan Unit was made against Miyagi. Before he could be arrested he cut his throat. It was a bad wound, but not likely to prove fatal with timely, competent attention. The man who believed he was dying confessed how the Japan Unit had operated and named the top five who directed it.

When Sorge took Kiyomi back to Tokyo the secret police arrested him. As he was taken into Colonel Osaki's office he saw some familiar scraps of paper on the desk. Colonel Osaki's men had performed painstakingly and well to recover the lost pieces of the message about Japanese intentions at Pearl Harbour. Before Osaki could speak Sorge said, 'I must remind you I'm a Soviet citizen and a lieutenant-general in the Soviet Army. I am to be treated with respect.' He did not add to those words, then or later. They were the last dignified words of a man who had reached his limit and faced personal disaster. He scorned a request to confess.

Klausen was caught and brought back and he confessed when the pressure was exerted, so did Hozumi Ozaki. Nearly fifty Communist helpers in the outer echelons of the Japan Unit were rounded up. One who refused to confess was de Voukelitch, who was reported to have preferred to join his ancestors.

Sorge continued in jail for months, the most important prisoner in Japan. He became bored and it was boredom that induced him to write his own fantastic story. But it was a slanted version of a twisted truth. It gave nothing useful to the enemies of the Soviet Union which had taken care not to share its information about Pearl Harbour with the Government of the United States.

With de Voukelitch keeping his ancestors company, only four of the five top members of the Japan Unit were brought to trial. Klausen and Miyagi, the latter's slashed throat now healed, were sentenced to fifteen years' imprisonment, Hozumi Ozaki and Richard Sorge received the death sentence. Ozaki took an hour and a half of excruciating punishment, with the steel ring being screwed into his neck very slowly, before he was dead; Sorge was hanged, or so it was claimed by the Japanese. But there were no witnesses, which was against Japanese precedent. On the day of the alleged hanging the new German Ambassador, Dr Heinrich Stahmer, reported to Berlin that the execution had been faked, to allow for Sorge's exchange for a number of

Japanese prisoners taken by the Russians in Siberia. This report was found by the Americans at the end of the war in the archives of the German Foreign Ministry. They also found another, which claimed that the vanished Richard Sorge had been appointed General Beldin's successor as the Fourth Bureau's chief. Since that time the legend of Richard Sorge has grown and changed in quality.

For instance, in 1947, when Kiyomi was appearing at the Seven Delights Club in Shanghai before a crowded audience of new post-war faces she stopped suddenly in a song and ran from the stage with a cry of fear. Some of the club's staff followed her into the street from a side-door and were only a few yards from her when three shots rang out. Kiyomi fell.

There was silence save for the sound of running feet. When Kiyomi was picked up she was dying. She did not recover consciousness or say who she had seen or why she had run in swift panic. But next day the rumour was rife in Tokyo: 'She was executed by Richard Sorge who had returned to take revenge.'

A man like Sorge, however, would have had a more impelling reason for returning to the Orient. In that same month of December 1947 the Chinese Communists were sweeping down from the north, and Shanghai lay directly in their advancing path. Was Sorge, if he had indeed been exchanged secretly, in China on a secret mission, perhaps creating a Soviet Communist cell to keep tabs on Maoist Communists, and had he undertaken that night to repay an outstanding personal debt? For all who hoped for proof, one way or the other, there has only been silence.